The Kingdom of Heaven is At Hand!

Biblical Principles for Appropriating the Kingdom Authority and Power!

SECOND EDITION

by

Dr. James Lee

God's Divine Deliverance Plans for the Israelites and Gentiles through the Son of David and the Son of Abraham

Published by
River of Life Ministries

ENDORSEMENTS

I have known Dr. James Lee since he was a student at the Regent University School of Divinity. In fact after we started the Doctor of Ministry program, he was one of the first to enroll and the very first one to graduate. It was an unforgettable moment for us to attend his dissertation defense that was arranged by the D. Min. Director, Dr. Russell West. Since that time, I have followed the career of Dr. Lee as he has worked tirelessly to expand the Kingdom of Jesus Christ around the world. We are truly grateful for all he has done.

This new book, *The Kingdom of Heaven is at Hand*, contains a concise and clear presentation of the entire Gospel story from Genesis to Revelation. It will go a long way to fill a need for such a book in the many Bible Schools and Mission Training Centers that Dr. Lee influences around the world. I wish Dr. Lee, his staff, and his worldwide River of Life Ministries the very best as he warns the world about the soon coming of Christ and the setting up of the eternal Kingdom which will never pass away.

Dr. Vinson Synan
Dean emeritus, Regent University School of Divinity
Virginia Beach, Virginia

Dr. James Lee is a master builder who has crafted a sure foundation in Jesus Christ and the revelation of God's Word, first in his life, then in the lives of multiple thousands around the world who have received his teachings and Holy Spirit empowered ministry. Now through this carefully written book we can all rejoice in making more and better disciples who can stand the shakings of these end times. Thank you Dr. Lee for your father-heart and apostolic mantle that you carry so caringly and sacrificially to the nations. We will stand on your shoulders to reach and serve those who are waiting for the truths in this book to establish their lives on the firm foundation that is revealed in these pages.

Dr. Joseph Umidi
Professor, Regent University
Virginia Beach, Virginia

Dr. Lee's relentless passion for God is evident on every page of his timely book, *The Kingdom of Heaven is at Hand.* Speaking as a fruitful revivalist, church planter and Bible teacher, he lays out the core teachings of the Kingdom of God that he has been proven worldwide firsthand throughout his years of ministry. It is balanced and powerful.

I particularly like the way Dr. Lee is both clear and concise in his writing. He grounds everything he says from careful exegesis, sound theology and church history. *The Kingdom of Heaven is at Hand* is a book that is both useful for the novice to the Faith and the mature saint. It will take every one deeper in their understanding of the kingdom and the ways of God. It is a treasure.

Dan Backens
Senior Pastor, New Life Providence Church

Virginia Beach, Virginia

Dr. James Lee has written a tremendous book clearly laying out the plan of salvation and how to grow in Kingdom life once a person has come to Christ as Lord. This book could be both a manual for believers helping them to better reach out to unsaved friends and family. It could also be an evangelistic tool for those needing more than just a Gospel tract to read for anyone serious about Kingdom life. I highly recommend it!

Clarence E. McPherson, Ph.D.
Senior Founding Pastor of Turning Point Church
Virginia Beach, Virginia

CONTENTS

INTRODUCTION

This book was written so that the Gentiles in the world are able to understand the true heart of the Creator of heaven and earth and to accept His salvation and kingdom plans for their lives. There is only one true God, and His personal name is "Yahweh" in the Bible. God's ultimate desire is to draw all men to Him so that whosoever calls upon the name of the Lord can be saved.

Israel has been God's special gift to the Gentiles in the world. Through the Son of Abraham and Son of David, God's chosen Jewish Messiah—Yeshua Ha-Mashiach (Jesus, the Messiah)—God provided the unique deliverance plan for the Gentiles to be adopted as the children of the Living God, who is the God of Abraham, Isaac, and Jacob. Without understanding God's divine **Salvation plan** through Abraham (Symbol is the Lamb of God.) and **Kingdom plan** through King David (Symbol is the Lion of Judah), the Jews and the Gentiles are not fully able to comprehend God's ultimate plan to save the fallen humanity.

Through activating God's divine salvation plan, Jesus conquered the power of sin, disease, curses, fear of death and Satan on the cross to set the suffering and dying souls free from the power of darkness. Through initiating His divine kingdom plan, Jesus received all authority in heaven and on earth (Matthew 28:18) to destroy the works of the devil (1 John 3:8b) and sent the power of the Holy Spirit to expand

His kingdom from Jerusalem to the end of the earth (Acts 1:8). May this simple book be used by God to destroy the dividing wall between the Jews and the Gentiles and to bring a new awareness of understanding the word of God in Genesis 12:1-3. Especially, verse 3 explains: *"And in you (Abram, the father of the Israelites), all the families of the earth (Gentiles) shall be blessed."* It has always been God's will to utilize His chosen people (the Israelites) to demonstrate His power, love, purpose, and plan to save the Gentiles in the nations of the world.

God's special Jewish people paved the way to usher in the Messiah so that He may provide the salvation plan for the Jews and Gentiles and establish the kingdom of God on earth. Without creating the Jewish nation and sending the Jewish Messiah, Yeshua, to take away the sins of the world, the Gentiles would never have a chance to be adopted as God's sons and daughters and to inherit the kingdom of heaven.

As a Gentile believer of the God of Abraham, Isaac, and Jacob, through Yeshua Ha-Mashiach, the Mediator between God and man, I am forever grateful to God's special Jewish people and their suffering to bring His divine salvation and kingdom plans for the lost world. When Yeshua of the Bible comes again to rule and reign over the kingdoms of the world, the children of God (the saints) whose sins have been washed by the blood of Yeshua will shine forever to usher in the King of Kings and the Lord of Lords (Matthew 13:43). The saints will judge the world and angels (1 Corinthians 6:2-3) and dwell in the new heaven and earth with the Lord forever, according to Revelation 21:1-5a:

> *And I saw a new heaven and a new earth, for the first heaven and the first earth had passed away. Also there was no more sea. Then I, John, saw the holy city, New Jerusalem, coming down out of heaven from*

*God, prepared as a bride adorned for her husband. And I heard a loud voice from heaven saying, **"Behold, the tabernacle of God is with men, and He will dwell with them, and they shall be His people, and God Himself will be with them and be their God.** And God will wipe away every tear from their eyes; there shall be no more death, nor sorrow, nor crying; and there shall be no more pain, for the former things have passed away." Then He who sat on the throne said, "Behold, I make all things new."*

Another reason I wrote this book was to share my discovery of God's heart for the world from Genesis to Revelation. The Bible describes the mission of the Triune God for fallen mankind. After searching for the meaning of life and answers to the question of life after death for a long time, I was introduced to the God of Abraham, Isaac, and Jacob in January 1977. Because of my Far Eastern upbringing in South Korea, the Bible and its teachings were very foreign religious matters to me at first.

However, it was fascinating and puzzling to discover that the first verse of the Old Testament begins with the statement, "In the beginning, God created the heavens and the earth." And the first verse of the New Testament begins with the genealogy of Jesus Christ as "the Son of David, the Son of Abraham." I asked myself, "Who are David and Abraham?"

As I continued to read the word of God, I discovered the special people group called "the Israelites" that God created for His own glory throughout the Bible. God made a covenant with the father of the Israelites, Abram (later changed to Abraham by God) in Genesis 12:3 and it was declared, *"And in you all the families of the earth shall be blessed."* The same covenant was repeated to his son, Isaac, in Genesis 26:4, *"...and in your seed all the nations of the earth shall be blessed."* Finally, the same God's covenant was also given to Abraham's grandson, Jacob, in Genesis 28:14, *"...and in you and in your seed all the families of the earth shall be blessed."* According to these Scriptures, it is very obvious that God created Abraham, Isaac, Jacob, and eventually the nation of Israel to bless all the families of the Gentiles in the world. The very purpose of creating the Israelites was for God to utilize them to release His divine blessing of salvation and kingdom plans for the Gentiles--all the families of the earth.

If God created the nation Israel to make Him known to all the families of the earth so that He could bless them, then the Israelites are God's special gift to the Gentiles of the world. As a Gentile believer of the Jewish God who is the Creator of the heavens and earth, I had a difficult time understanding the implications and meanings of many different events in the Bible, such as: the ritual sacrifice of lambs for the Passover, the Tabernacle and Ark of the Covenant, prophetic Scriptures for the coming of the Messiah, the Son of David and Son of Abraham, water baptism, the death and resurrection of Yeshua, the Messiah, the coming of the Holy Spirit, the Great Commission, the second coming of Yeshua to judge the world, the rapture of God's chosen people, the lake of fire, and much more.

After I became a follower of Yeshua and studied the word of God meticulously for 12 years, I began to understand the overall mission of the Bible. One day, my spiritual eyes were opened to a deeper understanding of many hidden secrets of the word of God. I began to discover that the Bible, from Genesis to Revelation, describes God's divine mission for fallen humanity. If you are one of the chosen Jewish people, you owe it to yourself to find out the mission of God in the Bible without having any biased opinions. The whole Bible revolves around the Jewish people, their origin, culture, patriarchs (Abraham, Isaac, and Jacob), Moses and the law of

God, Joshua, King David, the Temple, prophets, Yeshua, the, salvation and kingdom plans for the Jews and the Gentiles, and the end of the ages.

Ultimately, I discovered just how much the Jewish people and the nation of Israel are truly God's special gift for the Gentiles in the world. God has chosen His special people, the Israelites, through Abraham, Isaac, and Jacob, to provide His salvation plan for fallen mankind and His kingdom plan to reinstate them in His eternal kingdom on earth and in heaven. God created His physical kingdom (the Israelites) on earth to introduce His divine laws, statutes and commandments for His chosen people to obey and live by in the Old Testament times.

In the New Testament era, God provided His salvation plan through the Lamb of God who died on the cross to take away the sin of the world. God also initiated His kingdom plan through the Lion of Judah, Yeshua, the Messiah, who has risen from the dead, to provide the New Covenant to His spiritual kingdom (the Church or body of Christ) on earth through the Messianic Jews and Gentile believers.

I pray that this simple book will open the eyes of the Jewish people to realize that they are the gift to all the families of the earth. Therefore, the Jewish people are God's special bridge for the Gentiles to reconcile with the Creator—God of Abraham, Isaac, and Jacob—and to receive His divine salvation and kingdom plans to inherit the kingdom of heaven. This book covers the entire Bible from Genesis to Revelation in order to provide a complete picture of how God used the Israelites, His chosen people, to bring the Messiah, Yeshua, to provide God's secret plans to save the Jews and the Gentiles in the world, according to Isaiah 42:5-9:

> *Thus says God the Lord, who created the heavens and stretched them out, who spread for the earth and that*

which comes from it, who gives breath to the people on it, and spirit to those who walk on it: **I, the Lord, have called You in righteousness, and will hold Your hand; I will keep You and give You as a covenant to the people, as a light to the Gentiles,** *to open blind eyes, to bring out prisoners from the prison, those who sit in darkness from the prison house. I am the Lord, that is My name; and My glory I will not give to another, nor My praise to carved images. Behold, the former things have come to pass, and new things I declare; before they spring forth I tell you of them.*

Chapter 1

IN THE BEGINNING

❧

The Torah, known as the first five books of the Old Testament, begins in Genesis 1 and 2 with God's clear account of creating the sun, moon, stars, heaven, earth, every living thing, and human being. No other religious book in the world describes the creation of the world like the Torah. Only the Creator of the universe, heaven, earth, and all the things that are in it can give His divine details of the Creation in His own way in Genesis chapter 1. Here is a summary of the account of His creation in six days:

> *In the beginning, God created the heavens and the earth. The earth was without form, and void; and darkness was on the face of the deep. And the Spirit of God was hovering over the face of the waters. Then God said, "Let there be light"; and there was light... God called the light Day, and the darkness He called Night. So the evening and the morning were the __first day__... God made the firmament, and divided the waters which were under the firmament from the waters which were above the firmament... And God called the firmament Heaven. So the evening and the morning were the __second day__. Then God said, "Let the waters under the heavens be gathered together*

into one place, and let the dry land appear"; and it was so. **And God called the dry land Earth, and the gathering together of the waters He called Seas.** *And God saw that it was good.* **Then God said, "Let the earth bring forth grass, the herb that yields seed, and the fruit tree that yields fruit according to its kind,** *whose seed is in itself, on the earth"; and it was so... So the evening and the morning were the **third day**. Then God said, "Let there be lights in the firmament of the **heavens to divide the day from the night;** and let them be for signs and **seasons, and for days and years**... Then God made two great lights: the greater light to rule the day, and the lesser light to rule the night. **He made the stars also**... And God saw that it was good. So the evening and the morning were the **fourth day**. Then God said,* **"Let the waters abound with an abundance of living creatures, and let birds fly above the earth** *across the face of the firmament of the heavens." So the evening and the morning were the **fifth day**. Then God said, "Let the earth bring forth the living creature according to its kind: cattle and creeping thing and beast of the earth, each according to its kind"; and it was so... Then God said,* **"Let Us make man in Our image, according to Our likeness... So God created man in His own image; in the image of God He created him; male and female He created them.** *Then God blessed them, and God said to them,* **"Be fruitful and multiply; fill the earth and subdue it; have dominion** *over the fish of the sea, over the birds of the air, and* **over every living thing that moves on the earth...**" *Then God saw everything that He had made, and indeed it was very good. So the evening and the morning were the **sixth day**.*

Throughout human history, man-made religions and belief systems instigated the worship of the sun, moon, stars, heaven, mountains, and earthly objects such as statutes of men, animals, and religious figures, instead of the Creator who made them all. Created things, beings, and idols cannot give guidance to fallen mankind. Only the Creator, who has power over the living and dead, can truly provide His chosen people with His divine life on earth and eternal life in heaven. Any fallen sinner cannot provide the way, truth, and life to another sinner on this earth with his religious rituals. Only the holy and sinless God can provide His divine deliverance plan for fallen mankind. In this book, we will discover God's heart for the world as we unfold the whole connection of His divine deliverance plan throughout the Bible.

In Genesis 1:2, we discover **the direct involvement of the Spirit of God in the creation of the world**: *"The earth was without form, and void; and darkness was on the face of the deep. And **the Spirit of God** was hovering over the face of the waters."* It is very important to identify that the presence or appearance of the Holy Spirit precedes the creative work of God in His Creation. As the Spirit of God was hovering over the face of the waters, the earth was without form and void. Darkness was ready to receive God's light in Genesis 1:3, *"Then God said, 'Let there be light'; and there was light."*

Throughout the Bible, I discovered that the Spirit of God prepares the way of the Lord. This means God does not do anything without the presence and work of the Holy Spirit. When the Spirit of God appears or rests upon God's chosen vessel, He is ready to ignite His light into action to bring about God's divine intervention upon the troubled affairs of humanity. The Holy Spirit introduces God's special messages, purposes and plans to warn or deliver or guide His chosen people toward His perfect and divine direction throughout the Bible.

TRIUNE GOD (TRINITY)

At first, it was a very difficult concept for me to understand that the Lord has three distinct God-Persons who constitute and operate in unity as the Triune God. As I studied the word of God more intently, I was able to comprehend the divine concept of the Triune God (three God-Persons in One). The most important truth about the Triune God, though three distinct God-Persons exist, is that the Father, Son Yeshua, and the Holy Spirit work as one in absolute unity. Therefore, we can say that the Lord is one, according to Deuteronomy 6:4, *"Hear, O Israel: The Lord our God, the Lord is one!"* Yeshua (Jesus) confirms the same Scripture in Mark 12:29. Also, Isaiah 45:5a states, *"I am the Lord, and there is no other; there is no God besides Me."* The Apostle Paul describes in Galatians 3:20 that God is one. However, we also discover that God affirms the nature of the Triune God throughout the Bible.

The hint of the Triune God can be found in the first verse of the Torah, Genesis 1:1, *"In the beginning, God (Elohim) created...earth."* *"Elohim"* in Hebrew is a plural noun, implying God was not alone during creation. God clearly declares in Genesis 1:26, *"Let **Us** make man in **Our** image, according to **Our** likeness."* In this Scripture, we are able to identify that the Triune God (Father, Son Yeshua, and Holy Spirit) was involved in forming man from the dust of the ground. We have already discovered that the Holy Spirit was working with the Father God in His creation of heaven and earth. Now, we can also identify that the Son Yeshua was working with the Father God in creating the first human being. This statement can be verified by the Scripture in Colossians 1:16, *"For by Him (Yeshua or Jesus Christ) all things were created that are in heaven and that are on earth,* *visible and invisible, whether thrones or dominions or principalities or powers. All things were created through Him and for Him.*" What should be emphasized is that the Triune God (including Yeshua, the Messiah) was involved in creating mankind in Their image and likeness so that created man would shine the image and likeness of the Triune God in handling all different aspects of the affairs on this earth.

In the Old Testament, we can clearly identify the Triune God in Isaiah 48:16b, *"And now the Lord God and His Spirit have sent Me (Yeshua the Messiah)."* Also, Isaiah 61:1 says, *"The Spirit of the Lord God is upon Me (Yeshua the Messiah), because the Lord has anointed Me to preach good tidings to the poor."* In the New Testament, we can identify the Triune God more distinctively as in the name of the Father, Son, and Holy Spirit. When Yeshua was baptized by John, the Baptist, in Matthew 3:16-17, the Spirit of God alighted upon Him as the Father God spoke: *"Then Jesus, When He had been baptized, came up immediately from the water; and behold, the heavens were opened to Him, and He saw the Spirit of God descending like a dove and alighting upon Him. And suddenly a voice came from heaven, saying, 'This is My beloved Son, in whom I am well pleased.'"*

We can clearly see that the Triune God was manifested in action when Yeshua was baptized. The same account was described in Mark 1:9-11. The Triune God is identified in John 14:26 as well: *"But the Helper, the Holy Spirit, whom the Father will send in My (Yeshua) name, He will teach you all things, and bring to your remembrance all things that I said to you."* In Matthew 28:19, Yeshua commanded disciples to be baptized in the Triune God's name. *"Go therefore and make disciples of all the nations, baptizing them in the name of **the Father and of the Son and of the Holy Spirit**."* In 2 Corinthians 13:14, the Apostle Paul describes the Triune God in the following manner: *"The grace of the Lord Yeshua the*

Messiah (Jesus Christ), and the love of God (Father), and the communion of the Holy Spirit be with you all. Amen." It is very obvious that the Triune God has been in action throughout the Bible. The Father God mainly operated throughout the Old Testament through His appointed kings, priests, and prophets as they were inspired and anointed by the Holy Spirit to bring His divine directions to the Israelites. In the four gospels (the books of Matthew, Mark, Luke, and John), Yeshua the Messiah was led by the Holy Spirit (Luke 4:14) to bring the message and power of the kingdom of God. From the day of Pentecost in Acts 2, God the Holy Spirit has been in action through the believers or disciples of Yeshua to be His witnesses in Jerusalem, Judea and Samaria, and to the end of the earth (Acts 1:8).

It is not possible to accurately describe the complexity of the divine idea of the Triune God with any examples that we can find on this side of the earth. However, in my own understanding of the Triune God, it can be described as such: The Triune God can be compared to the makeup of a human person who is a triune being--spirit, soul, and flesh. Though one has three distinct parts within oneself, a human person is always recognized as one being with triune functions.

Therefore, 1 John 5:6-8 declares, *"This is He who came by water and blood--Yeshua the Messiah (Jesus Christ); not only by water, but by water and blood. And it is the Spirit who bears witness, because the Spirit is truth. For there are three that bear witness in heaven: the Father, the Word (Yeshua: John 1:1-5) and the Holy Spirit: and these three are one. And there are three that bear witness on earth: the Spirit, the water, and the blood; and these three agree as one."* It is very important for us to understand that Yeshua came to this world by the power of the Holy Spirit not only to bring the water, the absolute necessity of spiritual survival by washing and regenerating of our heart through the word of God, but also to provide the blood—life is in the blood. The blood of Yeshua cleanses us from our filthy sins and provides us with abundant life on earth and eternal life after death.

LET US MAKE MAN IN OUR IMAGE AND LIKENESS

The Triune God said in Genesis 1:26, "*Let Us make man in Our image, according to Our likeness.*" Merriam-Webster's Collegiate Dictionary defines "*image*" as "*a reproduction or imitation of the form of a person or thing; exact likeness; semblance; a tangible or visible representation, etc.*" It defines "*likeness*" as "*the quality or state of being like.*" Therefore, man was created to reproduce or imitate the tangible and visible form, attributes, character and qualities of the Triune God in managing, operating, and executing the affairs of the extension of the kingdom of heaven on earth. It was God's original intent to have very close communion with mankind in order to accomplish His plan and purpose through His chosen representatives—His special people who would shine His divine image and likeness on the earth.

God created male and female and commanded them to be fruitful and multiply, fill the earth and subdue it, and have dominion over every living thing that moves on the earth (Genesis 1:28). It was God's perfect will for man to have dominion and control over all of His creation on the earth by obeying His divine instruction, commandments, statutes, and missions. Therefore, God established a small extension of heaven in the Garden of Eden for His created mankind— Adam and Eve to enjoy the flawless environment where the presence of God dwelt with them. They lived in perfect harmony with the Creator who granted them His divine blessings, protection, eternal life, and dominion power to rule the earth. God walked with man, and man enjoyed His divine presence as His co-worker.

When God formed man of the dust of the ground (The Hebrew word for earth or ground is "*Adama.*" Thus, *Adam* was from *Adama.*), the Spirit of God breathed into man's nostrils the breath of life. Once the breath of life entered into the man's body, he became a living being (Genesis 2:7). God initiated divine life into His created man. Therefore life is a gift from God. Job 12:9-10 declares, "*Who among all these does not know that the hand of the Lord has done this, in whose hand is **the life of every living thing, and the breath of all mankind**?*" Also, King David writes in Psalm 36:9, "*For with You is the fountain of life; in Your light we see light.*" God has life in Himself, and He is the only One who can give life or take away life from His created beings.

Moses reinforced the concept that the Lord provides life to His obedient children in Deuteronomy 30:19-20, "*I call heaven and earth as witnesses today against you, that I have set before you life and death, blessing and cursing; therefore choose life, that both you and your descendants may live; that you may love the Lord your God, that you may obey His voice, and that you may cling to Him, for He is your life and the length of your days; and that you may dwell in the land which the Lord swore to your fathers, to Abraham, Isaac, and Jacob, to give them.*"

According to these Scriptures, mankind has been created and originated by the God of Abraham, Isaac, and Jacob, and the breath of life was a gift from Him. Thus, we can proclaim that mankind never evolved from the lowest form of an amoeba or a monkey. In contrast to the Evolution Theory, mankind was created in the image and likeness of the Creator, who breathed the breath of life into the body of man to make a living being (soul). God created all things beautiful and perfect, and mankind was His apex creation without any flaw and defect until sin entered into human life.

A HELPER COMPARABLE TO ADAM

God created every beast of the field and every bird of the air, as written in Genesis 2:19, *"Out of the ground the Lord God formed every beast of the field and every bird of the air, and brought them to Adam to see what he would call them. And whatever Adam called each living creature, that was its name."* Since God gave Adam power to have dominion over every living thing that moved on the earth (Genesis 1:28), He allowed Adam, His created man, to give names to every beast of the field. In a sense, God was inaugurating Adam to be His appointed ruler over His created animals on the earth as Adam gave them their names.

As Adam spoke the names of animals, their unique identities were established. Thus, from the beginning, God gave man His delegated power to proclaim, rule, and manage the affairs of every living thing on the earth. But for Adam, there was not found a helper comparable to him (Genesis 2:20). God created every beast of the field and every bird of the air out of the ground, including Adam. However, God created the final masterpiece--woman--out of the rib that He had taken from man (Genesis 2:21-23), and He brought her to Adam.

When Adam saw her, he called her *"Woman"* and didn't give her a personal name in the manner that he gave names to all other God's creation. She was simply called Woman because she was taken out of Man (Genesis 2:23). God gave the first man his distinctive name, *"Adam."* As mentioned, *"Adam"* means *"of the ground or taken out of the red earth,"* but Adam's wife didn't have her unique identity of her own name. One of the meanings of *"identity"* is *"the distinguishing character or personality of an individual."*

Every beast, bird, and fish was given a special name, except Adam's wife--woman. After Adam called his wife *"woman,"* the serpent called her *"woman"* in Genesis 3:1. Even God called her *"woman"* in Genesis 3:13, *"And the Lord God said to the woman."* Could it be that her lack of identity caused her to seek the attention of the serpent that opened a door for her to be tempted? Only after the fall did Adam give his wife a special name, *"Eve,"* which implied both her being the first mother of all living human beings and of the promised Seed who would sacrifice His life to provide salvation for the human race now subjected to death (Genesis 3:15).

Eve was created to be Adam's helper (*ezer* meaning *"to rescue, to save and to strengthen"*) in Genesis 2:18b, *"I will make him a helper comparable to him."* The Lord is recognized as *"Helper"* in Psalm 54:4, *"Behold, God is my helper (azar* meaning *"help, protect and supporting").*" and in Hebrews 13:6, *"The Lord is my helper (boethos* meaning *"to run to help"); I will not fear. What can man do to me?"* Also, the Holy Spirit is the Helper in accordance with John 14:16, *"And I will pray the Father, and He will give you another Helper (parakletos* meaning *"the One called to our side to help us, to stand by us, to strengthen us"), that He may abide with you forever."*

These three different designations of the term "helper" with the same meaning have been given to God, the Holy Spirit, and woman. Therefore, woman was created to be God's divine helper for man through hearing the guidance of the Helper—the Holy Spirit to rescue, to save and to strengthen Adam in all aspects of his mission on the earth as a co-partner in life.

In the Garden of Eden, Eve—as wife of Adam, didn't need to cook, wash dirty dishes after each meal, or launder clothing because they were freely allowed to eat all kinds of fruits in the Garden and they didn't wear any clothes. So what did her role as a helper consist of in the Garden, since she didn't really need to assist or help Adam with many household matters? She was probably called to help Adam with more spiritual matters led by the Holy Spirit—the Helper. However, she forfeited her role as Adam's helper when she allowed herself to be tempted by the devil and gave the forbidden fruit for Adam to eat as well.

In Adam's case, he was the one who originally received the commandment from the Lord not to eat the fruit of the tree of the knowledge of good and evil (Genesis 2:16-17) before Eve was created. Therefore, he should have been the one to forbid Eve from eating the forbidden fruit as her husband and the spiritual leader of their household. When both of them had fallen into sin, the judgment of God came down upon them. After the fall, Eve had to take care of many household duties, including cooking, cleaning, and washing all the days of her life. She also was sentenced to bringing forth children in pain. Furthermore, her desire became for her husband who began to rule over her in Genesis 3:16b, *"And you will desire to **control** your husband, but he will **rule** over you* (NLT)"

Regardless of what happened to man and woman after the fall, we need to understand God's original intention for male and female from the beginning. As we know, God created man (male and female) in His own image, according to Genesis 1:27, *"So God created man in His own image; in the image of God He created him; male and female He created them."* In the following verse 28, we can identify that God blessed them equally and said to them, *"Be fruitful and multiply; fill the earth and subdue it; have dominion over... every living thing that moves on the earth."* Therefore, God created male and female with His divine blessings so they could shine His image and likeness as they began to fulfill His commission in Genesis 1:28. Though Adam, the first male and husband, was created first before Eve, the first female and wife, the Creation mandate describes that male and female were created equally to fulfill God's divine purpose on the earth. This means, in terms of each male and female's position before God, the male was not created to be superior to the female or vice versa. As male and female became husband and wife before God, they were to respect, honor, and love each other as co-partners in life to glorify and fulfill God's divine plan for their lives.

However, even before the fall of mankind, God divinely ordained different functions to the male husband and female wife. It was God who appointed man (husband) to tend and keep the Garden of Eden (Genesis 2:15) and to keep His commandment in Genesis 2:16-17 before He created the woman (wife) in Genesis 2:21-22. Therefore, it is every husband's duty to be a spiritual leader in his own home to keep God's commandment and to love his wife as a partner in life. He also has a part in every spiritual, emotional, and physical need of his wife and children and must protect his family.

On the other hand, God created the wife as a best helper for her husband in order for him to fulfill His destiny for the family. She was created to provide any necessary support that her husband needs and to raise children to honor, respect, and fear the Lord and their earthly father. In this context, the wife's functional role is not any less honorable or important than the husband's or vice versa.

After the fall of mankind, the New Testament dictates and reinforces the same functional roles of the wife and husband in Ephesians 5:22-26, *"Wives, submit to your own husbands, as to the Lord. For the husband is head of the wife, as also*

Christ is head of the church; and He is the Savior of the body. Therefore, just as the church is subject to Christ, so let the wives be to their own husbands in everything. Husbands, love your wives, just as Christ also loved the church and gave Himself for her, that He might sanctify and cleanse her with the washing of water by the word." However, this does not mean that the husband is better or superior to the wife. They are equally created by God to serve Him as one unified body for His glory. Once a married couple is in Christ, a husband or wife's positional role before God has been justified as equal, according to Galatians 3:28b, *"...there is neither male nor female; for you are all one in Christ Jesus."* God divinely ordained His functional orders and rules in a home to be as He described in Ephesians 5:22-26. As we obey and respect God's divine rules for married relationships, His blessings will follow for those homes that abide by His instructions in any given functional marriage order.

In personal experiences of counseling numerous couples with marital problems in the United States and the rest of the world, I have never found a wife who was happy acting as the head of the home, taking care of everything because her husband was too passive or immature to take his ordained functional role, according to the word of God. On the other hand, no husbands were happy when their wives were very dominant and ruling and controlling the whole affairs of their homes.

GOD'S COMMANDMENT IN THE GARDEN OF EDEN

After God created Adam, Genesis 2:8-9 states, *"The Lord God planted a garden eastward in Eden, and there He put the man whom He had formed. And out of the ground the Lord God made every tree grow that is pleasant to the sight and good for food. The tree of life was also in the midst of the garden, and the tree of the knowledge of good and evil.*" It was God who created the Garden, which was the perfect environment where Adam and Eve were to enjoy His divine presence, life, blessings, health, provisions, joy, love, peace and protection. Adam was not required to assist God in establishing the Garden of Eden, but he was to tend and keep it (Genesis 2:15). By the same token, God created the earth and He put His mankind in it to tend and keep it according to His original intent, purpose and plan (Genesis 1:28).

In return, men ought to obey His laws, statutes, and commandments to keep the original environment of the earth to be filled with God's constant presence and glory. Ultimately, God created the heavens, earth, all the stars in heaven, all the living animals and plants, and human beings by His mighty power and for His pleasure and glory (Colossians 2:16). God is truly an omnipotent (having unlimited power), omnipresent (present everywhere at the same time) and omniscient (knowing everything) self-existing Being.

However, it is unbelievable that the created beings on earth sometimes act as though they are the creators and owners of the land, nations, peoples, tongues, and tribes in the world. The laws and commandments of God over His divine creations are completely disregarded. They even boldly declare that there is no God or that they would rather worship creatures, wooden or stone or steel idols, man-made philosophies, religions or religious idols or figures, doctrines, and ideologies as their guiding lights on the earth. We must repent of our own wicked ways and go back to the Creator God in order to reestablish an everlasting relationship with Him. Once we recognize the Creator as our one and only God through His divine Mediator—Yeshua, then He will bless us with His eternal life and empower us to expand His kingdom on earth with God's divine message of love. In the Garden of Eden, God gave only one commandment for Adam and Eve to obey. God declared that they would surely die if they disobeyed His commandment as written in Genesis 2:16-17, *"Of every tree of the garden you may freely eat; but of the tree of the knowledge of good and evil you shall not eat, for in the day that you eat of it you shall surely die."*

When God commanded Adam not to eat of the tree of the knowledge of good and evil, Eve was not yet created. Therefore, God mandated man, the spiritual leader of the household, to be responsible for keeping His commandment in the Garden of Eden. It was Adam's duty to instruct Eve to obey God's commandment after she was created to be his wife. Thus, even though Eve initiated the act of disobedience before God, He demanded an answer from Adam after the fall of man.

If Adam and Eve had obeyed God's commandment, they and their descendants would not have tasted physical death on the earth and eternal death in hell. God originally created human beings to live eternally as long as they would obey His commandments and keep His laws. It was God's absolute desire to allow His created humans to enjoy His presence, communion and unceasing fellowship on the earth as an extension of the kingdom of heaven. Thus, God initially provided two blessings for mankind:

Eternal life: As long as man obeyed God's commands in the Garden of Eden, he would have lived eternally. From the creation of mankind, God desired to have close communion with His created human beings if they demonstrated an obedient lifestyle before Him. However, even after man sinned before God and lost his divine privilege of eternal life on earth, God never altered His original plan for His chosen people. God initiated His deliverance plan to rescue those who would seek the Lord with repentant heart to accept His salvation plan. Those who accept God's salvation plan will enjoy eternal life in His paradise and eventually in the new earth (Revelation 21:1-5) before the presence of the Father, the Son (Yeshua), and the Holy Spirit forever and ever.

Authority or dominion power over every living thing: In other words, God wanted His created mankind to have divine authority over the living things in the world. It was God's absolute plan for man to rule over His created world through following His divine instructions, laws, statutes, and commandments so that the extension of the kingdom of heaven would be firmly established on the earth. The Lord, God of Abraham, Isaac, and Jacob, was, is, and always will be the King of Kings and the Lord of Lords on earth as it is in heaven. God has never forgotten or altered the fact that He gave His dominion power over the affairs of the earth to His chosen people. Eventually, the saints will rule the kingdoms of the earth with Yeshua, the Messiah, for a thousand years when He comes back again in the near future as the King of Kings and the Lord of Lords (Revelation 20).

As God gave Adam the power to have dominion over every living thing on the earth, he was given authority to name every beast of the field and every bird of the air (Genesis 2:19-20). God must have given Adam supernatural power to remember the names of every beast and bird on the earth. However, Adam was not able to find a helper comparable to him. So, the Lord God caused a deep sleep to fall on Adam, and He took one of his ribs and made it into a woman. Then He brought her to the man (Genesis 2:20-22). Just like God created a perfect helper for Adam and brought her to him, I believe that God will bring a perfect wife or husband to His chosen ones today so that they can be one with the Lord to fulfill His divine plan for their lives. After God brought a perfect helper to Adam, He gave a commandment for every married couple in Genesis 2:24, *"Therefore a **man** shall leave his father and mother and be joined to his **wife**, and they shall become one flesh."* The first institution that God created for mankind was the most sacred entity—family.

The very foundation of all other human institutions, including governmental, social, economical, political, and religious entities, is composed of a male or female who belongs to an integral part of a God-ordained family unit consisting of a husband (man), a wife (woman), and their children. When the very sacred fabric of marriage between a male husband and a female wife is altered apart from the perfect will of God, then the whole order of society will be imbalanced, and eventually it will destroy God ordained customs, culture, and foundation of marriage and the family unit in such a way that it will demolish the norm of a society.

If we willfully destroy the very first institution of God for mankind, we may invoke the same wrath of God to fall upon the society just like it did in Sodom and Gomorrah (Genesis 19:24-29). In the New Testament, the Apostle Paul states the matter even more clearly in 1 Corinthians 6:9-10, *"Do you not know that **the unrighteous will not inherit the kingdom of God**? Do not be deceived. Neither fornicators, nor idolaters, nor adulterers, **nor homosexuals, nor sodomites**, nor thieves, nor covetous, nor drunkards, nor revilers, nor extortioners will inherit the kingdom of God."* I am not the author of the above Scriptures, but the Lord is, and His law will stand firm regardless of how men or women try to justify their positions based on their own belief systems according to the worldly principles. God loves all sinners, but He hates sin because no one can inherit the kingdom of heaven if one's sins are not washed by the blood of the Lamb (Hebrews 9:22).

FALL OF SATAN

Satan is the personal name of the devil, meaning "slanderer" or "false accuser." The Bible does not describe exactly when Satan fell from his divine position as one of God's high-ranking angels. Perhaps he was one of the archangels in the kingdom of heaven. The following two Scripture passages describe the original position of Satan, who was once an angel called "Lucifer" in heaven, and the reasons and consequences of his fall:

How you are fallen from heaven, O Lucifer, son of the morning! How you are cut down to the ground, you who weakened the nations! For you have said in your heart: I will ascend into heaven, I will exalt my throne above the stars of God; I will also sit on the mount of the congregation on the farthest sides of the north; I will ascend above the heights of the clouds, I will be like the Most High. Yet you shall be brought down to Sheol, to the lowest depths of the Pit.
(Isaiah 14:12-15)

You were the seal of perfection, full of wisdom and perfect in beauty. You were in Eden, the garden of God; every precious stone was your covering... You were the anointed cherub who covers; I established you; you were on the holy mountain of God; you walked back and forth in the midst of fiery stones. You were perfect in your ways from the day you were created, till iniquity was found in you. Your heart was lifted up because of your beauty; you corrupted your wisdom for the sake of your splendor; I cast you to the ground, I laid you before kings, that they might

gaze at you. You defiled your sanctuaries by the multitude of your iniquities, by the iniquity of your trading; therefore I brought fire from your midst; it devoured you, and I turned you to ashes upon the earth in the sight of all who saw you. All who knew you among the peoples are astonished at you; **you have become a horror, and shall be no more forever.**
(Ezekiel 28:12b-13a; 14-15; 17-19)

According to these Scriptures, Lucifer fell from heaven because of the arrogance he held in his heart. Ultimately, Lucifer, a created angelic being, was filled with his own pride and agenda to become like the Most High God. His desire was to take over the control, management, and leadership of the affairs of the kingdom of heaven without submitting to and obeying the lordship of the King of Kings and the Lord of Lords. Before the fall of Satan, he was recognized as having the seal of perfection, being full of wisdom and being perfect in beauty.

However, when his heart was lifted up because of his beauty, God cast him to the ground as a profane thing. Satan was also present in Eden, the Garden of God, according to Ezekiel 28:13, *"You were in Eden, the garden of God; every precious stone was your covering."* Once Lucifer had fallen from his glorious position in heaven, he became determined to destroy God's divine love relationship with His marvelous creation, human beings, who were created after His own image and likeness. Satan also wanted to usurp God's two blessings of eternal life and authority that was given to mankind so that he could at least become the ruler of this world (John 12:31).

Since the fall of Satan, he became the great adversary of God and man. The devil means "accuser" or "slanderer" as revealed in Revelation 12:10b, *"...for* **the accuser of our** *brethren, who accused them before our God day and night, has been cast down."*

THE METHOD OF SATAN'S DECEPTION

It is not clear whether Satan was in the Garden of Eden before or shortly after the creation of Adam and Eve. Clearly, Satan was allowed to be in the Garden, and he knew God's commandment for Adam. After his fall, Satan devised a plan to cause man to disobey God's commandment so that he could destroy God ordained wonderful relationship between Himself and man. Once again, Satan's ultimate plan was to usurp the two blessings of man to take over the control of the affairs of the earth as its new ruler (John 12:31).

God originally created man to have eternal life on the earth just like the angels were created live eternally in heaven. However, Satan was determined to destroy God's blessings upon mankind. Satan knew that he didn't have any of his own power to cause man to lose God's two blessings or to bring death to mankind. Satan knew that if he could cause man to disobey God's one and only commandment in the Garden, then God's judgment and wrath ("...*for in the day that you eat of it, you shall surely die,*" Genesis 2:17) would surely fall on man.

God's every written word in the Bible will come to pass in its appointed time. Therefore, Satan's tactics against mankind have always been to cause man to disobey the laws, statutes, and commandments written in the Bible from God so that the curse, judgment, and wrath of God will fall upon disobedient mankind. Satan utilized three wicked methods to cause the woman to disobey God and to surrender her divine blessings to his evil plans: Distortion, Lies, and Manipulation.

DISTORTION: The definition of *"distort"* is *"to twist out of the true meaning or proportion."* Satan wanted to distort the true meaning of God's divine commandment to Adam and the woman in Genesis 2:16, *"Of every tree of the garden, you may freely eat."* When God clearly declared that Adam could freely eat of every tree of the Garden, except the tree of the knowledge of good and evil, Satan distorted the word of God and asked the woman to doubt what God said in Genesis 3:1, *"Has God indeed said, 'You shall not eat of every tree of the garden'?"* As Satan initially distorted what God commanded in Genesis 2:16-17 by asking a negative question concerning the same commandment, he was setting the stage to lead the woman further into his lying scheme through a dialogue.

The Bible states, *"The serpent (Satan) was more cunning than any beast of the field"* in Genesis 3:1. Satan, the once powerful angel known as Lucifer, lost his original abode in heaven and was outcast to the earth. However, he did not lose his wicked power, cruelty, shrewdness, craftiness, and evil intentions to deceive and to destroy God's apex creation—mankind. Thus, Satan continuously rebels against the Creator God and is determined to lead away as many human beings as he can from God's original plan of kingdom blessings to the eternal damnation in hell. Satan usually launches his wicked dialogue with his intended victim to cause doubt in his or her heart about the perfect will, plan, purpose, commandments, and ways that have been established in the word of God. Once anyone has engaged in a dialogue with Satan, he will be no match to the wicked craftiness of the deceiver. Instead of having a discussion with the devil, we need to flee from his wicked presence into the loving arms of the Lord for protection.

LIES: Even after the woman answered Satan's distorted question with a somewhat correct answer in Genesis 3:2-3, she began to ponder the question and reasoning of Satan in her heart. The woman didn't specify the tree which bore this fruit but explained how God described **the tree of the knowledge of good and evil** as the *"fruit of the tree which is in the midst of the Garden."* As the woman began to pay attention to his enticing, Satan boldly lied and stated his own word absolutely against what the Lord had commanded. When God said, *"You will surely die"* in Genesis 2:17, Satan twisted God's truth in Genesis 3:4 and lied and said, *"you will not surely die."* That was a direct contradiction to the word of God. At this juncture, Eve, the woman, might not have had the full awareness of the consequence of her sin that would bring death into her life and her descendants forever.

As she began answering Satan, the greatest tragedy of mankind began in Genesis 3:1-4, *"And he (Satan) said to the woman... And the woman said to the serpent (Satan)... Then the serpent said to the woman."* Once Satan successfully dialogued with the woman with a distorted question and enticed her with his wicked scheme, he was able to launch his best tactic of lying into her mind with a very crafty reasoning to cause a serious doubt in her heart about the word of God.

MANIPULATION: Once Satan's wicked schemes of distortion and lies infiltrated the woman's heart, he began to lead her into his deadliest plot. Satan undermined God's divine commandment that was established in her heart in order to deceive her with his evil tactic of manipulation. The meaning of *"manipulate"* is *"to control or plan upon by artful, unfair, or insidious means to one's own advantage; to change by artful or unfair means so as to serve one's purpose."* Satan wanted to manipulate God's word in the woman's heart so that he could accomplish his wicked purpose for his own advantage over mankind and the world. Now Satan directly manipulated mankind into achieving his own evil plan against

God and man. The Bible declares that Satan is a liar in John 8:44, *"You are of your father the devil, and the desires of your father you want to do. He (Satan) was a murderer from the beginning, and does not stand in the truth, because there is no truth in him. When he speaks a lie, he speaks from his own resources, for he is a liar and the father of it."* Satan was a murderer and liar from the beginning. However, Satan tried to make God a liar and manipulator by contradicting His statements in Genesis 2:17. As Satan tempted the woman with his final blow of the deadly manipulation, he suggested that God hid the blessings from her. The serpent manipulated her mind in Genesis 3:5, *"For God knows that in the day you eat of it your eyes will be opened, and you will be like God, knowing good and evil."*

   Satan's first manipulation: *"For God knows that in the day you eat of it, your eyes will be opened (Genesis 3:5a)."* Satan is implying that the woman's eyes were blinded to unknown pleasures and joys because she was forbidden to eat the fruit. The further implication of Satan's tactic was that God didn't want the woman's inner eyes to be exposed to the greater experience of her life. This is the same strategy that Satan uses to manipulate the young people of modern days to think that their inner eyes are closed to the greater experience of life in sex and pleasure when they are not allowed to taste the forbidden fruit.

   Satan tempts them not to listen to God's laws of abstinence or parental advice that seemingly deprive them of a deeper experience of life in sexual pleasure. However, once they have tasted the fruit, they are never the same before God and man forever. Their eyes are opened for the greater pleasures of exotic forbidden fruits. The same evil principle applies to drugs, gambling, pornography, cocaine, alcohol, nicotine, and any other addictions in a person's life.

Satan's second manipulation: *"...and you will be like God* (Genesis 3:5b)." Satan was suggesting that if the woman would eat the fruit, not only her eyes would be opened to hidden pleasures but also she would be like God. What was he implying to her? Satan was practically suggesting that the woman would be like God in such a way that she would not need to depend on God for her daily affairs. Satan was instilling in Eve's heart that she could be independent of obeying or following God's divine instruction, command-ments, statutes, judgments, directions, plans, purposes, and missions for her life. Thus, he was proposing to the woman that she could be her own master of her life apart from having the intimate relationship with the Creator. In this stage, Satan was injecting the most venomous poison, the spirits of rebellion, disobedience, independence, self-sufficiency, self-willed, self-centeredness, self-righteousness, etc. into her heart and mind.

Satan's third manipulation: *"...knowing good and evil* (Genesis 3:5b)." Satan was suggesting that the woman, as she became like God, would know good and evil by herself. Up to that point, the woman was sheltered by God's divine holiness, righteousness, love, joy, peace, and purity. She was perfectly protected from knowing and tasting evil. The woman knew the most wholesome goodness of God as she was enjoying the perfect and intimate relationship with the Creator God in the Garden of Eden. She probably wasn't even aware that there was such a force called "evil" in her life. Therefore, the most harmful enticement of the third manipulation was for the woman to discover evil in her life through committing the sin of disobedience against the perfect will and commandment of God in the Garden of Eden. Thus, Satan utilized three wicked tactics of distortion, lying, and manipulation to inject his poisonous sinful and rebellious natures into the woman's heart and mind so that she would disobey God's perfect will, plan, and purpose for her life. **Watch out! Satan will continuously tempt a person in these three ways to destroy his or her life from the perfect plan and purpose of God.**

What must we do when Satan's wicked temptations come into our lives? The best suggestion from God is written in the Book of James 4:7, "*Therefore submit to God. Resist the devil and he will flee from you.*" The first step is to repent of our rebellious and wicked ways before God. Secondly, we need to submit our will, motives, intentions, and plans to God and His divine instructions according to the word of God. Thirdly, we have to resist every temptation of the devil by claiming the truth in the Bible until Satan flees from us.

Chapter 2

FALL OF MAN

∽

Now it is important to examine how Eve, the woman, succumbed to Satan's wicked temptations. She was directly tempted in three different areas of her human weaknesses—1) physiological (flesh), 2) psychological (soul), and 3) spiritual (spirit) in Genesis 3:6, *"So when the woman saw that the tree was good for food, that it was pleasant to the eyes, and a tree desirable to make one wise, she took of its fruit and ate. She also gave to her husband with her, and he ate."*

First, Satan enticed the woman's weakness in her flesh. Once his temptation was able to penetrate into her fleshly desires, then he began to knock on her soul area where her emotions and feelings were dwelling. After breaking into her soul, Satan was able to launch his final attack into her spiritual area to bind her with his evil enticements. Ultimately, Satan was totally able to seduce her flesh, soul, and spirit to disobey and disregard God's commandment and to follow his wicked schemes to commit sin before God. However, if the woman would have rejected the temptations of Satan and asked the Lord to deliver her from his wicked plans, God would have rescued her, Adam, and their descendants from Satan, sin, curses, sicknesses and death forever. God created man to have freedom to choose what he desires with his free will. Therefore, God wanted His created human beings to obey and follow His commandments, statutes, laws, and plans through exercising their free will. The most powerful words that any man can ever say are "Yes" and "No." These words will bring immediate consequences after one chooses either "Yes" or "No" to any matter in life. For instance, if God would ask a man to follow Him so that He could reveal His divine plan to bless him and use his life to be a great blessing to multitudes of others, he has his free will to choose either to follow God's direction by responding "Yes" to His call or to reject Him by saying "No" to His plan. If the person says "No" to God, even though He has all power to force that person to obey Him, God will not induce the person to alter his own freewill to obey His call. However, if that person says "Yes" to God's call, then he will reap God's divine blessings for his life by obeying God's special plan.

By the same token, when Satan tempts a person to follow his wicked plans, that person has the power to say "Yes" or "No" to the devil's enticement. If the person firmly says "No" to Satan's evil plans and schemes and resists him, then the devil, though he has enormous evil power to coerce, cannot force the person to follow his satanic plans. However, if the person says "Yes" to Satan by exercising free will, then Satan can utilize all of his wicked power to bind the person to fulfill his wicked plans upon that person's life.

As one succumbs to Satan's temptation, the same fallen victim can influence multitudes of others to commit the same sin as well. Therefore, your "Yes" or "No" answer to your affairs will determine the course of your life in a positive way to produce a good fruit or a negative way to create a harmful or evil fruit. Thus, we must choose our "Yes" or "No" very wisely before we declare it. Because the woman chose "Yes" to the temptations of Satan in her flesh, soul, and spirit, she lost God's divine blessings in her life and opened a door to eternal death unto her and her descendants forever.

TEMPTATION IN PHYSIOLOGICAL (FLESH) AREA

"So when the woman saw that the tree was good for food...she took of its fruit and ate (Genesis 3:6)." After Eve, the woman, allowed the temptation of Satan to sink deep into her fleshly desire, she immediately began to look at the fruit and consider it to be good for satisfying her appetite. Once the woman's mind was made up to eat the fruit, she wasn't concerned about the commandment of God at all. While she was contemplating to eat the fruit, Satan's temptation had already been conceived in her flesh. In the same way, Satan's temptation will try to penetrate man's physiological area to cause its conception to take place. Once Satan has a victory over man's fleshly area, then his next step is to invade into man's psychological area where his emotions and feelings are dwelling.

Every living human being will always be exposed to some sort of fleshly temptations from the devil each day. That's why the Bible declares in Romans 3:23, *"...for all have sinned and fall short of the glory of God."* King Solomon went one step further and stated in Ecclesiastes 7:20: *"For there is not a just man on earth who does good and does not sin."* Also, the word of God states in Romans 7:5, *"For when we were in the flesh, the passions of sins which were aroused by the law were at work in our members to bear fruit to death."*

The Apostle Paul proclaims the works of the flesh more emphatically in 1 Corinthians 6:9-10, *"Do you not know that the unrighteous will not inherit the kingdom of God? Do not be deceived. Neither fornicators, nor idolaters, nor adulterers, nor homosexuals, nor sodomites, nor thieves, nor covetous, nor drunkards, nor revilers, nor extortioners will inherit the kingdom of God."* Also Romans 8:13 says, *"For if you live according to the flesh, you will die; but if by the Spirit you put to death the deeds of the body, you will live."* Therefore, we must not allow the devil's temptation to penetrate into our physiological area by putting to death the deeds of the flesh through the power of the Holy Spirit.

TEMPTATION IN PSYCHOLOGICAL (SOUL) AREA

"It was pleasant to the eyes (Genesis 3:6)." Once Eve, the woman, allowed the temptation to enter into her fleshly level, then she began to lose her footing in her soul through the door of her eyes. When the woman looked at the fruit, she exclaimed that it was pleasant to her eyes. By thinking this, Eve had already eaten the fruit in her mind; her sin had already been committed, just as Satan committed sin in his heart by saying the five "I will" statements in Isaiah 14:12-15 that caused him to be cast out of his glorified position in heaven. Yeshua (Jesus) declares that anyone who looks at a woman to lust for her has already committed adultery with her in his heart (Matthew 5:28).

The Bible describes that the lamp of the body is the eye in Matthew 6:22-23, *"If therefore your eye is good, your whole body will be full of light. But if your eye is bad, your whole body will be full of darkness. If therefore the light that is in you is darkness, how great is that darkness!"* Through our eyes, many temptations of the devil enter into our soul, and once sin has been conceived in our soul, it will produce evil fruits in our life. Therefore we must be very careful what we allow our eyes to see. Once our eyes allow sin to enter into our soul, then the Bible declares that our whole body will be full of darkness. Remember, Satan hatches his evil eggs in the darkness of our soul. The spiritual battleground of a man lies in his soul. In the Bible, the soul is described as the place of emotions and desires. Some examples are:

Desire for love in Song of Solomon 8:6-7, *"Set me as a seal upon your heart, as a seal upon your arm; for love is as strong as death, jealousy as cruel as the grave; its flames are flames of fire, a most vehement flame. Many waters cannot quench love, nor can the floods drown it. If a man would give for love all the wealth of his house, it would be utterly despised."*

Desire for food in Deuteronomy 12:20b & 21b, *"Because you long to eat meat, you may eat as much meat as your heart desires...and you may eat within your gates as much as your heart desire."*

Desire or longing for God in Psalm 63:1, *"O God, You are my God; early will I seek You; my soul thirsts for you; my flesh longs for you in a dry and thirsty land where there is no water."*

Emotion of rejoicing in Psalm 86:4, *"Rejoice the soul of Your servant, for to You, O Lord, I lift up my soul."*

Emotion or feeling of sorrow in Matthew 26:38, *"My soul is exceedingly sorrowful, even to death."*

Emotion of proceeding evil thoughts in Mark 7:21, *"For from within, out of the heart of men, proceed evil thoughts."*

Therefore, the word of God declares the importance of a man's soul in Mark 8:36-37, *"For what will it profit a man if he gains the whole world, and loses his own soul? Or what will a man give in exchanges for his soul?"*

TEMPTATION IN SPIRITUAL (SPIRIT) AREA

"A tree desirable to make one wise (Genesis 3:6).": Finally, the woman's soul was enticed with the lies of Satan, and then she also entertained the manipulation of the devil in the spiritual realm of her imagination. By this stage, the woman was fully bound by the distortion, lies, and manipulation of the devil in her flesh, soul, and spirit realms. The woman wanted to become like God, knowing good and evil for herself apart from depending on the Creator God for everything. The most tragic Scripture is written in Genesis 3:6b, *"She took its fruit and ate. She also gave to her husband with her, and he ate."* At least Adam, who received the commandment of God about the tree of the knowledge of good and evil before the woman was ever created, should have refused to take the fruit to eat. Before God brought the woman to Adam, he had a divine and holy relationship with his Creator God with absolute obedience in his heart.

However, Adam might have been so deeply in love with the woman that his loyalty, commitment, and dedication to God could have been divided between his affection for her and his Creator. Adam might have begun to love and honor his wife more than the Creator, so when she was tempted by Satan, he blindly and passively followed her suggestion into committing sin before God as well. Thus, Satan succeeded in causing the first of mankind to sin before God so that the judgment of the Creator in Genesis 3:16-19 would fall on every human descendant on the earth from that day forward. Man will continuously be tempted in these three ways. After Adam and the woman sinned, they tried to cover their nakedness with fig leaves. Likewise, when we commit sin, we will also try to cover our sin with our self-righteous coverings. For example, we might blame other people, circumstances, situations, our childhood upbringing, our parents, husbands, wives, children, the devil, and even God for the result of our sinful acts.

The devil will first tempt a man in his physical or fleshly realm with wicked schemes. Once a man is enticed by the desires of the flesh, the devil will then penetrate into the psychological or soul realm to manipulate his emotion, mind, and heart. Eventually the devil will invade the spiritual realm of a man to alter his virtue, will, moral standing and integrity to make him follow the devil's wicked schemes (Satan's temptation → flesh → soul → spirit). However, when God regenerates a person, He first works on his or her spiritual realm to transform the inner spiritual being through convicting power of the Holy Spirit. Once a person is willing to yield his or her spirit to the guidance of the Holy Spirit, God will then influence his or her soul (mind) area to be renewed so as him or her to follow the righteous way of God. Lastly, God will cause the most vulnerable and sinful fleshly part of a person to be submitted to the perfect will of God (God's regeneration work → spirit → soul → flesh).

RESPONSIBILITY OF ADAM (THE FIRST HUSBAND)

Even though it was Eve, the woman, who committed sin before God, God questioned Adam about it because He had given the commandment to him first. God told Adam that he should not eat of the tree of the knowledge of good and evil in Genesis 2:16-17 well before He ever created the woman. Therefore, God wanted Adam to be responsible for the fall of mankind because He appointed Adam to be the spiritual head of the household to tend and keep the Garden of Eden

(Genesis 2:15). Adam was not only to tend and keep the Garden but also to instruct his wife to follow God's law according to His order, direction, and commandment. Thus, Adam was the steward who was responsible for operating, managing, and overseeing the Garden as God's representative on the earth. Eve was created to help and assist Adam to obey, follow, and execute God's direction, vision, and mission in life fulfilling her positional and functional roles as an equal partner and a perfect helper.

Throughout the Bible, God declares that the earth and those who dwell in it belong to the Lord: *"The earth is the Lord's, and all its fullness, the world and those who dwell therein. For He has founded it upon the seas, and established it upon the waters* (Psalm 24:1-2)." *"For the pillars of the earth are the Lord's, and He has set the world upon them* (1 Samuel 2:8c)." *"Heaven is My throne, and earth is My footstool* (Isaiah 66:1a)."

If the earth and those who dwell in it belong to the Lord, then every human being who has ever lived on the earth must be a good steward of the given territory where God has appointed him or her to dwell for the appointed time. Thus, God reasoned with Adam after the fall in Genesis 3:11b, *"Have you (Adam) eaten from the tree of which I commanded you that you should not eat?"* However, Adam blamed God for his sin in Genesis 3:12, *"The woman whom You gave to be with me, she gave me of the tree, and I ate."*

Adam was almost implying that God gave him the wrong wife. In reality, it didn't matter who gave the forbidden fruit to him. If Adam truly feared the Lord, he shouldn't have eaten it. In God's eyes, a passive sinner is as guilty as the one who initiates to commit sin. As the first husband forfeited his responsibility and blamed God and his wife for his downfall, the same generational curse has been passed on to every husband. One time or another, every husband will blame, condemn, or judge his wife for his own failures or have a critical spirit to pass his fault on to his wife; or he may even blame God for providing him with the wrong wife. However, a husband needs to remember that God requires the head of the household to be responsible for anything that goes wrong under his roof because it is the husband's ultimate duty to tend and keep his own garden according to God's love, commandment, laws, and statutes just as a head of the body is absolutely concerned about the welfare of every part of his physical being.

Therefore, every husband must take the full responsibility for the consequences of sins, failures and downfalls that are occurring in his own household before God, even if he believes that it is his wife's fault. God will always ask the husband, the spiritual leader of the house, to answer for any shortfalls happening in his household regardless of who may have instigated them. When we sin, we need to humble ourselves before the Lord and sincerely repent of our sins and not blame anyone else. Our sincere repentant heart before God will invoke His forgiveness according to 1 John 1:9, *"If we confess our sins, He is faithful and just to forgive us our sins and to cleanse us from all unrighteousness."*

When the first Adam sinned before God, he relinquished his position of authority on the earth to Satan who, by default, became "the ruler of this world" according to the word of Jesus Christ in John 12:31 and 16:11. Thus, Satan was able to usurp the two authorities or blessings (eternal life and authority to rule the world) that were given to mankind. But the last Adam (Jesus Christ) came to restore the original plan for His chosen people who would accept Him as their Messiah, Lord and Savior:

Eternal life: Originally, man was created to live eternally; however, when he disobeyed God, the judgment of God in

49

Genesis 2:17 came down upon every human descendant and every human being began to die on this earth since the first death of Abel in Genesis 4:8. The first obituary notes of the deceased people are recorded in Genesis Chapter 5.

Authority to rule the world: God gave Adam the authority to have dominion over every living thing that moves on the earth in Genesis 1:28. However, when he sinned before God, Satan became the ruler of this world (John 16:11) to unleash his wicked plans; such as murder, violence, hate, jealousy, sexual immorality, war, famine, destruction, disease, unforgiveness, bitterness, anger, and curses to bind God's apex creatures, human beings with his wicked evil power.

ADAM! WHERE ARE YOU?

Immediately after Adam and Eve sinned before God, the first thing that they realized was that their eyes were open to know good and evil for themselves, and they knew that they were naked. Before the fall, I believe that the glory and presence of God surrounded them in such a marvelous way that they didn't recognize that they were naked. They only knew the holiness, glory, blessing, love, joy, peace, power, wisdom, splendor, goodness and constant presence of God in the Garden of Eden.

They were in God ordained perfect environment. However, sin separated them from the attributes of God as Isaiah 59:1-2 states: *"Behold, the Lord's hand is not shortened, that it cannot save; nor His ear heavy, that it cannot hear. But your iniquities have separated you from your God; and your sins have hidden His face from you, so that He will not hear."*

Once they were aware of their nakedness, they tried to cover themselves with fig leaves in Genesis 3:7, *"Then the eyes of both of them were opened, and they knew that they were naked; and they sewed fig leaves together and made themselves coverings."* The result of their disobedience was the loss of innocence and the new awareness of knowing the knowledge of good and evil for themselves. Just like Adam and Eve did, when we sin, we will try to cover our own sinful nakedness with our own device instead of seeking the Lord's forgiveness and His divine remission for sins. Not only did they realize that they were naked but also they tried to hide themselves from the presence of God as seen in Genesis 3:8, *"And they heard the sound of the Lord God walking in the garden in the cool of the day, and Adam and his wife hid themselves from* **the presence of the Lord** *God among the trees of the garden."* It was the vivid revealing of the most tragic condition of the fallen mankind.

Adam should have led the woman, his wife, back to the Lord, their Maker, with a penitent heart and asked God's divine forgiveness for forsaking His commandment. One can only wonder if Adam and the woman had repented of their sins in the Garden, what the outcome might have been for the descendants of mankind after them. Unfortunately, they ran away and hid themselves from the presence of God. Every sinner has the same nature of Adam in his blood in such a way that he or she always wants to find many excuses to run away and hide from God and His people because His presence will utterly expose any sin within him or her.

Instead of the first sinner and fallen man, Adam, calling upon the Lord and asking for His forgiveness, it was God who initiated to look for him in Genesis 3:9, *"Then the Lord God called to Adam and said to him, 'Where are you?'"* Ever since the first call of God for the lost sinner, Adam, He has been calling the fallen sinners—"Where are you?" **God is also**

calling you now. Where are you? As you begin to acknowledge Him by saying, "Here am I, Lord!" God will guide you to know the truth of His salvation and kingdom plans. **Don't stop now. Today, find a new life in Yeshua (Jesus Christ) and live for the glory of God. God loves you and has a mighty plan for your life on the earth and in heaven for eternity. Regardless of the sinful situations that you have been in so far, God has power to set you free from the bondage of the devil and give you a brand-new life, hope, and future if you will only turn to Him, repent of your wicked ways (any ways that are not in line with God's ways that are described in the word of God) and call upon His name—even NOW!**

Chapter 3

GOD'S INITIATION OF THE DELIVERANCE PLAN

~~~

Before Adam and Eve committed sin before God, they enjoyed a very intimate relationship with God in the perfect environment in the Garden. However, after they sinned, they hid themselves from the presence of God (Genesis 3:8). It is a great tragedy to know that Adam not only hid himself from God but also became afraid of Him as illustrated in Genesis 3:10, *"I heard Your voice in the garden, and I was afraid because I was naked; and I hid myself."* When God questioned Adam if he had eaten from the tree of which He commanded him not to, Adam blamed his wife for his own sin. When God confronted Eve about the sin, she blamed the serpent (Satan) for deceiving her.

The fall of man brought physical and spiritual deaths upon the descendants of Adam forever and caused them to lose the two divine blessings of God—eternal life and dominion power over every living thing on the earth. The most tragic outcome was the fact that Satan usurped the two blessings that were given to mankind and became the prince of the power of the air (Ephesians 2:2), the ruler of this world (John 16:11), and the god of this age (2 Corinthians 4:4). However, God didn't alter or change His original intentions for mankind, regardless of what the devil had done against them. Immediately after the fall of man, even though Adam and Eve didn't repent of their sins before God, He initiated His divine deliverance plan to rescue fallen mankind—all of the human descendants of Adam and Eve—from sin, sickness, curse, fear of death, and the power of Satan in Genesis 3:15, *"And I will put enmity between you and the woman, and between your seed and her Seed; He shall bruise your head, and you shall bruise His heel."*

This is one of the most important prophetic messages about the coming of the Messiah in the Torah and the whole Bible. This Scripture predicts that someday the Seed (Yeshua the Messiah or Jesus Christ) of the woman (God's chosen people—the future nation of Israel) will come and bruise or crush the head of the serpent (Satan). Satan will bruise His heel that will be accomplished on the Cross. Nevertheless, Yeshua will rise again to provide God's salvation and kingdom plans for fallen mankind. It is very important to notice that the nation of Israel and His chosen people were not yet created; however, He already planned to bring the Messiah through the woman—the Israelites—to save not only the Jews but also the Gentiles in the world.

The most important fact that Jewish people need to understand at this point is that the Lord (Yahweh or Elohim or El Shaddai), originated His divine deliverance plan to be available for the descendants of Adam and Eve—the whole fallen mankind of all nations, peoples, tribes and tongues including the Jews. The first book of the Torah in Genesis 10 describes the names of the nations descended from Noah before the nation of Israel was ever formed. However, in order for God to initiate His divine salvation and kingdom plans for fallen mankind, He created His missionary nation, Israel, to reveal His divine laws, statutes, commandments, and His replica theocratic kingdom on earth.

This would eventually usher in the Messiah (Yeshua), the Seed of the woman, to crush the head of the devil to open up the door to the spiritual kingdom of God to the Jews and the Gentiles of the world. Therefore, we can confirm that God will send His Messiah through the nation of Israel as the light to the Gentiles, according to Isaiah 42:6b-8, *"I will keep You (Yeshua the Messiah) and give You as a covenant to the people, as a light to the Gentiles, to open blind eyes, to bring out prisoners from the prison, those who sit in darkness from the prison house. I am the Lord, that is My name; and My glory I will not give to another, nor My praise to carved images."*

GOD'S TWO DELIVERANCE PLANS

Immediately after the fall of man, God activated His perfect deliverance plan through the chosen Seed (His own Son, Yeshua the Messiah) who would be born in Israel in His divine time as the Son of Abraham to become the universal Savior for the descendants of Adam in Genesis 3:15. However, in order for God to provide the Savior for all mankind, He had to create His chosen people who would recognize the one and only Creator God (Yahweh) as their Lord to obey and follow His commandments, laws, and statutes as His chosen kingdom on the earth. Thus, God initiated two plans—the **kingdom plan** and **salvation plan**-- that declare Yeshua is the Messiah for all mankind. We will discuss these plans throughout this book, but let's take an initial look at them.

KINGDOM PLAN: God never deviated from His original plan for mankind that He commanded to the first man, Adam, in Genesis 1:28, *"Be fruitful and multiply; fill the earth and subdue it; have dominion over the fish of the sea, over the birds of the air, and over every living thing that moves on the earth."* It was always God's perfect will for man to have His authority on the earth to rule over every living thing by maintaining a perfect relationship with Him. Satan knew the original plan of God for mankind, so he had to usurp the authority of man on earth by using the evil tactics of deception, lies, and manipulation that caused Adam to sin against God.

The fall of man caused Satan to become "the ruler of this world" (John 12:31), "the god of this age" (2 Corinthians 4:4), and "the prince of the power of the air" (Ephesians 2:2). Nevertheless, immediately after the fall of man, God began to initiate His divine deliverance plan (Genesis 3:15) in order to reestablish His kingdom on earth through His chosen people, the Israelites, who would obey His laws, principles, statutes, rules, and commandments.

His divine plan included rescuing fallen mankind from eternal damnation of hell and at same time destroying the works of the devil—sin, curses, sickness, fear of death, perversion, sexual immorality, idolatry, poverty, slavery, demonic bondages, etc. on the earth. The first plan was to create the nation of Israel (the woman in Genesis 3:15) through Abraham's descendants.

Eventually, God would establish the prototype theocratic kingdom on earth through King David to manifest His kingdom plan to all mankind. Therefore, Yahweh, the Creator God, declared to King David in 2 Samuel 7:16, *"And your (King David) house and **your kingdom shall be established forever** before you. **Your throne shall be established forever.**"* Throughout the Old Testament, the Kingdom of David was the model kingdom on earth. David was a righteous king who obeyed the commandments, laws, statutes and judgments of God with all his heart. During his kingship over Israel, he always recognized the true King, Yahweh, as his Lord and Master over his life and the affairs of the kingdom of Israel. Even though the physical kingdom of David had ended before the end of the Old Testament era, Yahweh hadn't forgotten about His promise to King David and His chosen people of Israel. God sent His own Son, Yeshua, to be born as the Son of David (Matthew 1:1), who was the Lion of the tribe of Judah (Revelation 5:5), to fulfill His spiritual kingdom plan on the earth as it was prophesied in Isaiah 9:6-7 and Luke 1:32-33:

> *For unto us a **Child** is born, unto us a **Son** is given; and the government will be upon His shoulder, and His name will be called Wonderful, Counselor, **Mighty God, Everlasting Father**, Prince of Peace. Of the increase of His government and peace there will be no end, upon **the throne of David and over His kingdom**, to order it and establish it with judgment and justice from that time forward, even forever.*
> (Isaiah 9:6-7)
> *He will be great, and will be called the Son of the Highest; and **the Lord God will give Him the throne of His father David**. And He will reign over the house of Jacob forever, and **of His kingdom there will be no end**.* (Luke 1:32-33)

When Yeshua was crucified on the cross to take away the sin of the world, He died as **the Lamb of God, the Son of Abraham, to provide God's perfect salvation plan for all mankind.** However, when Yeshua rose from the grave, He was resurrected not as the resurrected Lamb of God but **as the Lion of Judah to sit on the throne of David to establish the Spiritual kingdom of David on the earth.** He crushed the head of the serpent and defeated him as the prince of this world. From that time on, Yeshua the Messiah became the King of Kings and the Lord of the Lords to usher in the eternal kingdom plan for His chosen people who would be raised from every nation, people, tongue, and tribe in the world. These new people of God will have only one King, Yeshua, and His divine kingdom on earth that declares Yahweh (the personal name of God) as their only Lord. Yahweh is also called as Elohim (All-Powerful One, Creator), El Shaddai (All-Sufficient One, God Almighty), Adonai (Lord, Great God), El Elyon (God Most High), and El Olam (Eternal, Everlasting God). The ultimate dominion of the whole earth by the spiritual kingdom of God would be ruled by the Son of Man (Yeshua the Messiah), that was also prophesied in Daniel 2:34-35; 7:13-14:

> *You watched while a Stone was cut out without hands, which struck the image on its feet of iron and clay, and broke them in pieces. Then the iron, the clay, the bronze, the silver, and the gold were crushed together, and became like chaff from the summer threshing floors; the wind carried them away so that no trace of them was found. And the Stone that struck the image became a great mountain and filled the whole earth.*
>
> (Daniel 2:34-35)
>
> *I was watching in the night visions, and behold, One like the Son of Man, coming with the clouds of heaven! He came to the Ancient of Days, and they brought Him near before Him. Then to Him (Yeshua the Messiah) was given dominion and glory and a kingdom, that all peoples, nations, and languages should serve Him. His dominion is an everlasting dominion, which shall not pass away, and His kingdom the one which shall not be destroyed.*
>
> (Daniel 7:13-14)

According to the prophetic Scriptures, the spiritual kingdom of God was inaugurated on the earth as Yeshua was crucified on the cross as the Lamb of God, rose from the grave as the Lion of Judah, and ascended to heaven to sit on the right-hand side of Yahweh, Father God. When God the Holy Spirit came down upon the believers (new sons and daughters of the Living God) to initiate the kingdom work on the earth, according to Acts 1:8 and Matthew 28:18-20, the kingdom power had been released to believers of Yeshua to expand the kingdom of God throughout the world. Since that time, there has been an epic clash between the kingdom of darkness and the advancement of the kingdom of God as described in Matthew 11:12, *"And from the days of John the Baptist until now the kingdom of heaven suffers violence, and the violent take it by force."*

The Bible relates the purpose of the coming of the Son of God in 1 John 3:8, *"He who sins is of the devil, for the devil has sinned from the beginning. **For this purpose the Son of God was manifested, that He might destroy the works of the devil.**"* This is why Yeshua commanded His disciples to preach the kingdom of heaven and to demonstrate kingdom power in His name to destroy the works of the devil in Matthew 10:7-8, *"And as you go, preach, saying, 'The kingdom of heaven is at hand.' Heal the sick, cleanse the lepers, raise the dead, cast out demons. Freely you have received, freely give."*

Therefore, when the kingdom of heaven invades this world, the power of the Holy Spirit will destroy the works of devil in the name of Yeshua. This means, the Church must not only preach the salvation message of Yeshua but also demonstrate His kingdom power to heal the sick, cleanse the lepers, raise the dead, and cast out demons whenever we gather in His name.

SALVATION PLAN: In order to implement the salvation plan, God has to create the nation of Israel (the woman in Genesis 3:15) through Abraham so that God could bless all the families of the earth through Abraham's descendants according to Genesis 12:3, *"And in you (Abraham) all the families of the earth shall be blessed."* God provided His divine universal deliverance plan (meaning His kingdom and salvation plans are applicable to all humanity) for fallen mankind not only for the Jews but also for all nations, tribes, peoples, and tongues (Revelation 7:9-10).

God originally created his apex creation—mankind—to live eternally in Paradise called the Garden of Eden and to have dominion over every living thing on the earth as God's direct representatives, rulers, or ambassadors. In this Paradise, men enjoyed a perfect relationship with the Creator God who provided for and blessed them with everything in the purest and perfect form without having any fear of sin, death, sickness, curse and poverty.

Therefore, it was never God's intention for mankind to live in a world that has been infested, perverted, cursed, diseased, and polluted with sin, sickness, violence, and fear of death from Satan's wicked evil schemes. The current conditions of the world began to manifest to the inhabitants of the earth after Adam and Eve fell into the temptation of the devil and were cast out from the presence of the Creator God, Yahweh. For the consequence of their sin, the judgment of God fell upon them and their descendants forever. The Bible declares that the wages of sin is death in Romans 6:23 and describes two kinds of death:

Physical death on the earth: Every living being will eventually die either by natural or by unnatural means. Before the Flood, men lived up to nine hundred plus years; however, God limited man's life span to one hundred twenty years in

Genesis 6:3, *"My Spirit shall not strive with man forever, for he is indeed flesh; yet his days shall be one hundred and twenty years."* It was further reduced to seventy-to-eighty years in Psalm 90:10, *"The days of our lives are seventy years; and if by reason of strength they are eighty years."* Even though men were originally created to live eternally, the wages of sin brought death upon all men since Adam's sin. That means every man must experience the pain, sorrow, and agony of death when our earthly lives are over.

Eternal death in hell: Many modern-day Jews and some gentiles believe that physical hell does not exist. Physical hell is a real place, according to the following Scriptures: Deuteronomy 32:22, *"For a fire is kindled in My anger, and shall burn to the lowest hell; it shall consume the earth with her increase."* Psalm 9:17, *"The wicked shall be turned into hell, and all the nations that forget God."* Psalm 55:15, *"Let death seize them; let them go down alive into hell."* Proverbs 15:24, *"The way of life winds upward for the wise, that he may turn away from hell below."* Isaiah 14:9, *"Hell from beneath is excited about you, to meet you at your coming; it stirs up the dead for you."*

Matthew 10:28, *"And do not fear those who kill the body but cannot kill the soul. But rather fear Him who is able to destroy both soul and body in hell."* Mark 9:43, *"If your hand causes you to sin, cut it off. It is better for you to enter into life maimed, than having two hands, to go to hell, into the fire that shall never be quenched."* Therefore, after physical death on the earth, you will have to face eternal death in hell if your sins are not forgiven by the blood of Yeshua the Messiah.

After the fall of man, every human being who has been born into this sinful world inherited the curse of the first man: physical and spiritual death. This means, since the fall of man, all human beings who have ever been born into this world have inherited the curse of death as well as other curses, such as diseases, poverty, rebellion, violence, murder, sexual immorality, war, famine, starvation, perversion, and others. In order for God to pardon the sin of any man, an innocent animal had to shed its blood and die on behalf of a sinner during the Old Testament days. However, the atonement for sin in the Old Testament days was only a temporary measure to cover sin of a man for a year. The Israelites had to bring their sacrificial animals each year to the High Priest to receive their forgiveness of sins, especially on the day of Yom Kippur, the Day of Atonement (Leviticus 16:8-10, 20-22, 29-34).

None of the Old Testament practices of sacrificing the blood of animals to atone the sin of the Israelites before the Almighty, Righteous and Holy God were ever sufficient to appease Him. Therefore, Father God Himself decided to provide His own eternal and permanent sacrifice—His own Son Yeshua who is the perfect sinless Son of Man as well as the perfect Son of God—to die on the cross during the week of Passover as the final Passover Lamb to take away the sin of the world. That's why John the Baptist called Yeshua (Jesus) "the Lamb of God" in John 1:29, "*Behold! The Lamb of God who takes away the sin of the world!*"

Through the salvation plan, God provided the sacrificial Lamb to atone for the sins of all mankind just like He demonstrated the covering of the sins of Adam and Eve in the Garden with animal tunics. In order for the Son of God to be born as the Seed of the woman in Genesis 3:15, He had to be born as the Son of Abraham, who birthed the nation of Israel—the woman, to fulfill the prophetic word of God to Abraham in Genesis 12:3, "*And in you (Abraham) all the families of the earth shall be blessed.*" Therefore, the first verse of the New Testament, Matthew 1:1, begins with the most important statement in the whole Bible: "*The book of the genealogy of Jesus Christ (Yeshua the Messiah), the Son of David, the Son of Abraham.*" As the Son of Abraham, Yeshua—the Lamb of God, brought the message of universal salvation for all mankind as He shed His own blood on the cross to save fallen humanity from sin, sickness, curses, death, and the power of Satan.

GOD'S CURSE UPON THE SERPENT AND JUDGMENT ON WOMAN AND MAN

After the fall of man, the consequence of sin or the curse of God came down upon Adam, the woman, and the serpent. The Bible clearly states that the wages of sin is death (Romans 6:23). Also, James 1:13-15 declares clearly how one can be tempted: *"Let no one say when he is tempted, 'I am tempted by God'; for God cannot be tempted by evil, nor does He Himself tempt anyone. But each one is tempted when he is drawn away by his own desires and enticed. Then, when desire has conceived, it gives birth to sin; and sin, when it is full-grown, brings forth death."*

Not only sin will invoke death, but it will also open the door for curses (the fruit of sin) to be activated in your life. One of the most important facts that we need to understand at this point is that death and curses were initiated by the Creator God and not by Satan. Lucifer was God's angelic creature in heaven. When Lucifer sinned before God and was cast out into the earth, he became the devil, the serpent, or Satan (Isaiah 14:12-15). In a way, Satan cannot bring death or curses upon humans in his own accord or power.

Furthermore, Satan has no power to bring even one soul of man into hell in his own accord. Only the Creator of heaven and earth and of all the things that are in them has the power to bring death, curses, and eternal destruction to any mankind. This is why we need to fear the Lord who has power to destroy both soul and body in hell according to Matthew 10:28, *"And do not fear those who kill the body but cannot kill the soul. But rather fear Him (Creator God) who is able to destroy both soul and body in hell."* However, Satan knows that if he will tempt man to sin against God, then the judgments of God that are written in the Bible will be activated against the sinner. Satan also knows that he has been already condemned to eternal damnation in the lake of fire without ever having a chance for redemption. Therefore, Satan's ultimate desire is to take as many humans as he can to the lake of fire with him according to Revelation 20:11-15.

In order to fulfill his evil desire, Satan has been continuously enticing mankind to sin against the law, statutes, and commandments of God so that the judgment and curses of God can fall upon them. Once any man sins against God and falls into the temptation of the devil, then he becomes a slave of Satan to be ruled, tormented, used and abused by his wicked evil schemes. For a righteous man to be directly afflicted by Satan, the devil had to acquire God's permission just as it was described in Job 1:6-12, specifically in verse 12, *"And the Lord said to Satan, 'Behold, all that he has is in your power; only do not lay a hand on his person.'"* So Satan went out of the presence of God with His permission to afflict a blameless and upright man, Job, with wicked devices.

THE SERPENT WAS CURSED

A great physical change took place in the serpent after the curse pronounced in Genesis 3:14, *"Because you have done this, you are cursed more than all cattle, and more than every beast of the field; on your belly you shall go, and you shall eat dust all the days of your life."* Genesis 3:15 proclaimed that the Seed of the woman would eventually crush the serpent's head. However, the greatest curse that had fallen upon Satan was the day that he lost his status as one of the most perfect and beautiful angels and was cast out of the kingdom of heaven to the earth, according to Revelation 12:7-9:

> *And war broke out in heaven: Michael and his angels fought against the dragon; and the dragon and his angels fought, but they did not prevail, nor was a place found for them in heaven any longer. So the great dragon was cast out, that serpent of old, called the Devil and Satan, who deceives the whole world; he was cast to the earth, and his angels were cast out with him.*

Satan was not only cast out of heaven but also cursed by God on the earth. Eventually, he will be cast into the lake of fire according to Revelation 20:10, *"The devil, who deceived them, was cast into the lake of fire and brimstone where the beast and the false prophet are. And they will be tormented day and night forever and ever."*

THE WOMAN WAS CONDEMNED

Truly, the woman lost her divine blessings in the Garden of Eden. While she was living in the perfect paradise, she didn't need to cook or clean or feel any pain. However, when she sinned before God, the consequences of sin such as death, sorrow, pain, sickness and submission to her own husband, fell upon her as long as she would live on the earth according to Genesis 3:16, *"I will sharpen the pain of your pregnancy, and in pain you will give birth. And you will desire to control your husband, but he will rule over you. (NLT)"*

One of the greatest dilemmas in any woman's married life is the conflict between her husband's wish to rule over her and her own desire to control her husband in relation to who will manage the internal affairs of a home. There is only one way that a woman can be delivered from the condition of the curse—when she surrenders her life to Yeshua as her Lord and Savior and lives her life in peace with God and man through the power of the Holy Spirit. Even though her pain in childbearing will not disappear, she can raise godly children by training them to obey the instruction of the Bible. As she follows the examples in Proverbs 31, her own husband and children will respect her at home. God will bless her and use her for expanding the kingdom of God on earth as His special vessel.

THE MAN WAS CONDEMNED

The ground is cursed, and in toil, man will eat the fruit of it all the days of his life. As Adam sinned, spiritual death that separated man from the presence of God came upon all mankind. Ultimately, he will physically die and return to dust, according to Genesis 3:17b-19:

> *Cursed is the ground for your sake; in toil you shall eat of it all the days of your life. Both thorns and thistles it shall bring forth for you, and you shall eat the herb of the field. In the sweat of your face you shall eat bread till you return to the ground. For out of it you were taken; for dust you are, and to dust you shall return.*

Consequently, the devil, the beast, false prophets, and anyone whose name is not written in the Book of Life will be cast into the lake of fire (Revelation 20:10, 15). Afterward, these curses upon whole mankind will be abolished in Revelation 22:3-4, *"And there shall be no more curse, but the throne of God and of the Lamb shall be in it, and His servants shall serve Him. They shall see His face, and His name shall be on their foreheads."* However, prior to Revelation 22:3, those who have accepted the redeeming work of Yeshua, the Messiah, on the Cross and have had their sins cleansed by the blood of the Lamb of God will be set free from the curse of the law in accordance with Galatians 3:13, *"Christ has redeemed us from the curse of the law, having become a curse for us (for it is written, 'Cursed is everyone who hangs on a tree'), that the blessing of Abraham might come upon the Gentiles in Christ Jesus, that we might receive the promise of the Spirit through faith."* The death of Yeshua on the cross also abolished the curses (including generational curses) upon anyone who has become a child of God through the remission of sin by the blood of the Lamb.

INITIATION OF THE SUBSTITUTIONAL SACRIFICE

After the fall, God had a dilemma with Adam and Eve in the Garden of Eden. There was the tree of life in the midst of the Garden. If they would eat the fruit from the tree of life, they would live forever in their sinful state without having any hope of redemption from God (Genesis 3:22-24). Furthermore, the whole of cursed humanity would also have to be cast into the lake of fire with Satan, demons, and false prophets because the wages of sin is death (Revelation 19:20; 20:14; Romans 6:23). However, in order for God to save the fallen mankind, He initiated the divine deliverance plan to rescue His chosen people from their sins, curses, sickness, poverty, death, and Satan's destructive power on the earth. God had to drive them out of the Garden of Eden. Before God cast them out of the Garden, He clothed them with tunics of skin in Genesis 3:21. This was the first incident God had to kill innocent animals to cover Adam and Eve's nakedness and sins. Adam and Eve had to watch innocent animals (perhaps lambs) bleeding and dying in order for God to atone for their sins. Therefore, the first sacrifice of "substitutional" animals occurred in the Garden of Eden. This is the beginning of the atonement practices of shedding innocent blood of animals in the Old Testament.

Therefore, God allowed the sacrificial death of an animal to symbolize two important facts: 1) Sin brought death upon all mankind on the earth. 2) The practice of atonement and covering of man's sin by substitutional animal's blood began. The word of God declares in Leviticus 17:11, *"For the life of the flesh is in the blood."* From this point on, every human being who was, is, and will be born into the world was infected with the sinful nature of Adam and Eve. And everyone's sin must be atoned for by the sacrificial blood of the substitutional animal throughout the Old Testament and by the blood of the Lamb of God in the New Testament era.

Thus, the word of God declares in Romans 3:23, *"for all have sinned and fall short of the glory of God."* This means all men need to accept God's divine deliverance plan for their lives in order to avoid the judgment of God because the wages of sin is death, according to Romans 6:23, *"For the wages of sin is death, but the gift of God is eternal life in Messiah Yeshua our Lord."* Furthermore, the Bible pronounces that the remission of sin requires the shedding of innocent blood in Romans 9:22, *"And according to the law almost all things are purified with blood, and without shedding of blood there is no remission."*

THE SHADOW OF DEATH UPON MANKIND

God's judgment, which was pronounced upon mankind in Genesis 2:17 came upon Adam, Eve, and their descendants forever beginning in Genesis 4:8, *"Cain rose against Abel his brother and killed him."* The first death that was ever recorded in the Bible was the animals that God killed in the Garden of Eden to cover the nakedness of Adam, and the second event was the death of Abel, a son of Adam and Eve. The first death of man was the result of Cain becoming angry with God because his offering was not respected but Abel's was. Cain's anger turned into a murderous act of jealousy against his brother Abel who didn't do anything wrong to Cain.

While Cain was filled with anger toward God and jealousy against his brother, God began to speak with him in Genesis 4:6-7, *"So the Lord said to Cain, 'Why are you angry?' And why has your countenance fallen? If you do well, will you not be accepted? And if you do not do well, **sin lies at the door. And its desire is for you, but you should rule over it.**"* Since we all inherited Adam's sinful nature, we should also rule over sin and sinful desires that would lie at the door of the path of our life. If we do not rule over sin, then sin will enslave us with passion, lust, corruption, perversion, sexual immorality, destruction, and other ills.

In this account, we can clearly see Cain's rebellious heart toward Yahweh. He not only didn't obey the instruction of the Lord but also disregarded His instruction to rule over the desire of sin in his heart. The result was a very tragic one. Cain's disobedient heart caused him to be angry at God, and his sinful desire instigated him to kill his own brother instead of repenting of his sins before the Lord. Therefore, Adam and Eve had to face the first death of their beloved son, Abel, and experience the pain of separation from their murderous son,

Cain. Adam and Eve lost both of their first two sons and truly began to witness the fulfillment of God's Word in Genesis 2:17, "*...you shall surely die.*"

Genesis 5 is nothing but the obituaries of mankind from Adam to Lamech. Genesis 5:5 states, "*So all the days that Adam lived were nine hundred and thirty years: and he died.*" Since the death of the first man, Adam, all mankind began to die. As we said, before the Flood in Genesis Chapter 7, people lived over 900 years. Methuselah lived 969 years (Genesis 5:27). However long they lived on the earth, at the end, they all died. Furthermore, the Creator God decided to terminate the human race from Adam to Noah's generation because of their great wickedness, as recorded in Genesis 6:5-7:

> *Then the Lord saw that the wickedness of man was great in the earth, and that every intent of the thoughts of his heart was only evil continually. And the Lord was sorry that He had made man on the earth, and He was grieved in His heart. So the Lord said, "I will destroy man whom I have created from the face of the earth, both man and beast, creeping thing and birds of the air, for I am sorry that I have made them."*

Through the Great Flood, God terminated all His first creations except Noah and his family and the chosen animals (Genesis 7:11-24). However, God prepared the ark to spare His chosen seed to repopulate the earth with His divine New Covenant (Genesis 8:21):

> *And all flesh died that moved on the earth: birds and cattle and beasts and every creeping thing that creeps on the earth, and every man. All in whose nostrils was the breath of the spirit of life, all that was on the dry land, died. So He destroyed all living things which*

were on the face of the ground: both man and cattle, creeping thing and bird of the air. They were destroyed from the earth. Only Noah and those who were with him in the ark remained alive" (Genesis 7:21-23). "I will never again curse the ground for man's sake, although the imagination of man's heart is evil from his youth; nor will I again destroy every living thing as I have done." (Genesis 8:21)

Truly, death visited every living being on the face of the earth as Romans 6:23 states, *"For the wages of sin is death."* However, for the righteous ones before God, He will always provide His divine ark to preserve them from His wrath and destruction.

THE TOWER OF BABEL, THE FIRST ORGANIZED AND MAN-MADE RELIGION

Mankind, once again, began to rebel against God and tried to make a name for itself in Genesis 11:4, *"Come, let us build ourselves a city, and a tower whose top is in the heavens; let us make a name for ourselves, lest we be scattered abroad over the face of the whole earth."* During those days, the whole earth had one language and one speech. This was the way for men to reach up to God with their own means and ideas to make a name for themselves and not for the glory of God. This is the foundation for man-made religions of the world. There is no way man can reach up to God with his own devices, regardless of how religious it may appear. God also knew that His created mankind could do anything if all spoke one language and united as one body as written in Genesis 11:6, *"And the Lord said, 'Indeed the people are one and they all have one language, and this is what they begin to do; now nothing that they propose to do will be withheld from them.'"* Therefore, God confused their language and scattered them abroad over the face of all the earth as seen in Genesis 11:7-9:

> *Come, let Us go down and there confuse their language, that they may not understand one another's speech. So the Lord scattered them abroad from there over the face of all the earth, and they ceased building the city. Therefore its name is called Babel, because there the Lord confused the language of all the earth; and from there the Lord scattered them abroad over the face of all the earth.*

God didn't want men to organize any religions, religious activities, religious tower, or idols to reach up to Him with rituals, traditions, sacrifices, idol worship, or the false fear of Him. All of the organized religions of the world try to provide their own ways to reach up to the Creator through the practice of many different rituals and formalities. None of the religious books of the world begins as the Torah and Old Testament Bible: *"In the beginning God created the heavens and the earth..."* or *"Then God said, 'Let there be light' and there was light..."* or *"Then God made two great lights: the greater light to rule the day, and the lesser light to rule the night. He made the stars also..."* or *"Then God said, 'Let the earth bring forth the living creature according to its kind; and it was so..."* or *"Then God said, 'Let Us (the Father, the Son and the Holy Spirit) make man in Our image, according to Our likeness..."*

The reason that other religious books cannot begin the first chapter with the same statements as the Bible is because they depict men's ideas, religious views, philosophies, and ways to reach up to heaven where the Creator dwells. However, the Torah is the Book of the Creator God that conveys the messages of how He created the universe, stars, sun, moon, and every living thing on the earth. Furthermore, other religions in the world require men to sacrifice their lives for their gods, but the Creator God initiates His divine deliverance plan to provide His only Son, Yeshua, to die on the Cross for the sin of the world as His divine sacrificial Lamb of God, according to His prophetic word in Genesis 3:15. Therefore, since God's call to Adam in Genesis 3:9, it is God who has been calling fallen humanity back to Himself—the essence of God's deliverance plan.

Chapter 4

THE ABRAHAMIC COVENANT
(The Salvation Plan)

~∞~

Once again God was in action to create a brand-new people group for Himself through a pagan man from the land of Ur of the Chaldeans. According to Joshua 24:2, "*Your fathers, including Terah, the father of Abraham and the father of Nahor, dwelt on the other side of the River in old times; and they served other gods.*" Abraham served other gods until God called him to follow Him in Genesis 12:1-3. God was in motion to fulfill His prophetic word that He spoke to the serpent in Genesis 3:15. We need to remember that God was always thinking about providing the universal deliverance or salvation plan for all of fallen mankind and not just for one specific people group in the world.

However, in order for the Creator God (Yahweh) to initiate His own deliverance plan for all humanity, He had to create a special people group who would know Him in a very personal, unique, and real way as His own chosen people. God's intention was to establish a chosen people group who would worship and serve the One and Only Creator of the heavens and the earth and all the things in it. While all other people groups in the world were worshiping idols, God began to create His special people group, the Israelites, through His chosen couple, Abraham and Sarah. God began to equip and train Abraham and Sarah to establish a special nation that would obey and follow all of His statutes, laws, commandments, and judgments so that the rest of the nations of the world would know that there was the One and only Living God who dwelled with the Israelites. Therefore, if we carefully examine the call of Abram in Genesis 12:1-3, we will clearly understand that it was His divine plan to make His blessings available to all the families of the earth.

God created the Israelites to let the whole world know of His divine deliverance plans—the kingdom and salvation plans. This means God's overarching intention for the Israelites was, is, and always will be to become the fountainhead of blessing to all nations, tribes, peoples, and tongues in the world. However, throughout the history of the Israelites, the Jews had the true but unhealthy identity of themselves as the chosen people of God and looked down upon the Gentiles as the people groups they should not associate with. As a result, the Jews hardly accepted or understood the true call and purpose of their creation—***In you all the families of the earth shall be blessed.***

God made three distinct promises to Abraham and his descendants in Genesis 12:1-3:

> *Now the Lord had said to Abram: "Get out of your country, from your family and from your father's house, to a land that I will show you. I will make you a great nation; I will bless you and make your name great; and you shall be a blessing. I will bless those who bless you, and I will curse him who curses you;* ***and in you all the families of the earth shall be blessed.***"

1) I will make you **a great nation**.
2) I will **bless you**.
3) You shall be a blessing (Key)
Results: **And in you all the families of the earth (the Gentiles) shall be blessed**.

The first two blessings were to be fulfilled by the Lord Himself. However, in the third part, God was asking Abram to be a blessing to all the families of the earth. This has to be obeyed by Abram and his descendants forever. The Lord, Yahweh the Creator of heaven and the earth, throughout the history of the nation of Israel had freely given the top two blessings to the Israelites whenever they would obey the commandments of Him. The Israelites always had a special call to share the truth of knowing the One and Only True Living God and His divine deliverance plan to all the families of the earth. For this very purpose, the Lord called Abram to create His special people on the earth.

Therefore, God had to take Abram out of his own country and family because they were worshiping other gods (idols). God wanted Abram to initiate a new beginning that would cause him to know the Creator and His divine mission for his life. If Abram didn't obey God's call upon His life, He would have had to choose someone else to fulfill His mission for creating a chosen people that would become the blessing to all the families of the earth. God had to set Abram apart for His divine purpose and plan so that He could use him to fulfill His deliverance plan for fallen mankind. Consequently, the call of Abram to create God's specially chosen people, the Israelites, was to bless the rest of the families of the earth through His eternal deliverance plan that was prophesied in Genesis 3:15.

Once Abram obeyed God's commandment and came to the land of Canaan with his wife Sarai, his nephew Lot, and servants, the Lord appeared to Abram in Genesis 12:7 and said to him: *"To your descendants I will give this land. And there he built an altar to the Lord, who had appeared to him."* The second most important covenant that God promised to Abram was to give the land of Canaan to his descendants forever. Abram began to call on the name of the Lord, Yahweh (Genesis 12:8) and not any other pagan idols. Thus, God began the new beginning with His chosen man Abram to create the new people of God who would call upon His name as His chosen people group. It was the beginning of the new people group called the Israelites.

GOD'S COVENANT WITH ABRAHAM

God made a covenant with Abram and said in Genesis 17:4-5, *"You shall be a father of many nations. No longer shall your name be called Abram, but your name shall be Abraham; for I have made you a father of many nations."* God changed the name Abram to Abraham in order to make His call upon him clear and to make Abraham to be a father of many nations and not just for the one nation of Israel. It was God's perfect plan to establish the nation of Israel to bless the whole world. God truly established a great nation out of the descendants of Abraham and blessed them exceedingly.

However, His ultimate purpose for creating Israel was to utilize Jewish people to bless all the families of the Gentile world. Thus, the Apostle Paul declares in Galatians 3:8 that Genesis 12:3 was the first gospel recorded in the whole Bible: *"And the Scripture, foreseeing that God would justify the nations by faith, preached the gospel to Abraham beforehand, saying, 'In you all the nations shall be blessed.'"* Eventually the Messiah, the Savior of the world, was born as the descendant of Abraham (Matthew 1:1) and the Seed of the woman (Israel), according to Genesis 3:15, to be the blessing unto all the families of the earth. Thus, whosoever calls upon the name of the Lord the Messiah (Jesus Christ) shall be saved and given the power to become a child of God through Abraham. Therefore, God's covenant with Abraham in Genesis 12:3 was fulfilled through the Son of Abraham, the Messiah Yeshua, the Lamb of God, who takes away the sin of the world (John 1:29) and the Lion of Judah who sits on the throne of David, and His kingdom will be no end (Luke 1:32-33).

God repeated His covenant with Abraham in Genesis 12:3 to Isaac in Genesis 26:4-5 and to Jacob in Genesis 28:14. From then on, His name is called "*the God of Abraham, the God of Isaac, and the God of Jacob.*" Why does He have to name all three of the patriarchs to affirm His name? If God would have simply stated that He was only the God of Abraham, then His chosen seed Isaac and his descendants, as well as a natural seed of Ishmael and his descendants, would be included as the chosen people. If God would have stated that He was only the God of Abraham and the God of Isaac, then even though the descendants of Ishmael had been eliminated from the line of the chosen people, Isaac's two descendants, Jacob as well as Esau whose descendants became the Edomites, would have been included.

Therefore, when God says that He is the God of Abraham, the God of Isaac, and the God of Jacob, then only His chosen people and descendants from the 12 tribes of Israel (Jacob), Isaac, and Abraham are included as His special covenant people of God. It was very obvious that God separated His chosen people very clearly from other people groups in the Old Testament days. Even in the New Testament era, those who have accepted the Messiah Yeshua (Son of David and Son of Abraham) as their only Lord and Savior, by believing His sacrificial death on the cross for the remission of their sins, are qualified and blessed to become children of the Creator God. Once again, God's divine purpose for His chosen people is to set them apart so as to shine His light, law, commandments, statutes and life to the Gentiles of the world.

MELCHIZEDEK, THE PRIEST OF GOD MOST HIGH

Before the initiation of the Levitical order of the high priest in Leviticus 16, Abraham recognized Melchizedek as the priest of God Most High and gave him a tithe of all his goods in Genesis 14:18-20. This same event is described in Hebrews 7:1-3. Melchizedek, who had been called king of righteousness and king of Salem, meaning *"king of peace,"* was described in Hebrews 7:3 as *"without father, without mother, without genealogy, having neither beginning of days nor end of life, but made like the Son of God, remains a priest continually."* God was already setting up the precedent to establish the eternal High Priest for all mankind someday so that the prototype of high priests in the Old Testament would be expanded to all the families of the earth.

The formal priesthood in Israel began in Exodus when the Levites were chosen to carry out the priestly duties throughout the Old Testament days. One of the most important duties of the high priest was to stand in the gap between God and the Israelites as His mediator to perform all the rituals of sacrificing animals to provide the covering for their sins. The high priest would sprinkle the blood of sacrificial animals on the altar and the mercy seat of the Ark of the Covenant on behalf of the Israelites to mediate God's atoning grace for them. In the Old Testament days, there were many priests, because they were prevented by death from continuing.

However the Messiah Yeshua, who died on the Cross as the final Lamb of God, sprinkled His own blood on the heavenly Mercy Seat once and forever to atone not only for the sins of the Israelites but also for the sins of all the Gentile families of the world. Because He was resurrected from the grave as the King of Kings and the Lord of Lords to live forever, He has an unchangeable priesthood. Thus, God established Yeshua as the eternal High Priest according to the order of Melchizedek:

> *Therefore, if perfection were through the Levitical priesthood, what further need was there that another priest should rise according to the order of Melchizedek, and not be called according to the order of Aaron? For He of whom these things are spoken belongs to another tribe, from which no man has officiated at the altar. For it is evident that our Lord arose from Judah, of which tribe Moses spoke nothing concerning priesthood. And it is yet far more evident if, in the likeness of Melchizedek, there arises another priest who has come, not according to the law of a fleshly commandment, but according to the power of an endless life.* (Hebrews 7:11-16)

THE PASSOVER

God made a covenant with Abraham in Genesis 15:5 and said, *"Look now toward heaven, and count the stars if you are able to number them. So shall your descendants be."* However, the Omnipotent, Omnipresent, and Omniscient God forewarned Abraham what would happen to his descendants in a foreign land in Genesis 15:13-14, *"Know certainly that your descendants will be strangers in a land that is not theirs, and will serve them, and they will afflict them four hundred years. And also the nation whom they serve I will judge; afterward they shall come out with great possessions.*"

Before a great famine came upon the land of Canaan, God sent Joseph (Genesis 37-47) to Egypt ahead of Abraham, Isaac, and Jacob's descendants to prepare the way for them to be preserved during the great famine. In due season, Joseph became the second man in power after Pharaoh in Egypt. As long as Joseph was in power, the Israelites received special treatment and favor from Pharaoh. However, Exodus 1:6-7 describes, "*And Joseph died, all his brothers, and all that generation. But the children of Israel were fruitful and increased abundantly, multiplied and grew exceedingly mighty and the land was filled with them.*"

When the new king who did not know Joseph arose in Egypt, he began to afflict them with heavy burdens. Even the king of Egypt commanded Hebrew midwives, who ended up not obeying the king, to kill the sons of the Israelites in Exodus 1:16, "*When you do the duties of a midwife for the Hebrew women, and see them on the birth stools, if it is a son, then you shall kill him; but if it is a daughter, then she shall live.*" After the Israelites had endured 430 years (Exodus 12:40) of Egyptian bondage, God raised Moses to deliver them from their slavery. God inflicted Egypt with ten different plagues in order to force Pharaoh to let the Israelites go. God spoke to Moses in Exodus 8:1, "*Go to Pharaoh and say to him, 'Thus says the Lord: Let My people go, that they may serve Me.*'"

While the Israelites were under the bondage of Egyptian slavery, they were not able to serve the Creator God. In a way, Egypt was the incubator to birth the nation Israel. The whole people group of slaves was about to become the chosen nation called Israel ("Prince of God"). The final plague, which demonstrated God's ultimate power and caused Pharaoh to let the Israelites go, was the death of all the firstborn sons in Egypt (Exodus 11:1 - 12:36). In order to protect the Israelites from the His last judgment against Egyptians, God gave the very specific instruction of His divine protection plan for the Israelites to Moses. God commanded Moses to instruct the Israelites to kill a lamb per household and apply the blood (the innocent blood of the lamb) to the two doorposts and the lintel of the houses (Exodus 12) in order to protect their first-born male child from death as recorded in Exodus 12:23, *"For the Lord will pass through to strike the Egyptians; and when He sees the blood on the lintel and on the door posts, the Lord will pass over the door and not allow the destroyer to come into your houses to strike you."*

God's instruction for selecting a Passover lamb was very specific in Exodus 12:5-6. *"Your lamb shall be without blemish, a male of the first year. You may take it from the sheep or from the goats. Now you shall keep it until the fourteenth day of the same month. Then the whole assembly of the congregation of Israel shall kill it at twilight."* The lamb was to be taken out from the flock on the tenth day of Nisan and kept until the fourteenth day of the month. As families kept a lamb for four days among themselves, they would be attached to it as their own lamb. They would feel the loss of their lambs and understand the cost of the sacrificial lamb to die on behalf of their sins.

The Passover was the two-edged sword. One side was to destroy every first-born male child in Egypt as the final judgment of God, and the other side was to kill innocent lambs to protect the seed of His chosen people from destruction. In order for the sin of the Israelites to be forgiven, numerous innocent lambs had to be sacrificed throughout the Old Testament days. The Passover ceremony became one of the most important events throughout the history of Jewish people. In the New Covenant, Yeshua partook His last

Passover with His disciples in Luke 22:7-20 as the final Passover Lamb. He would introduce His divine salvation plan for all the families of the world to fulfill the prophecy in Genesis 12:3 as He shed His own blood on the Cross after He spent three and a half years (compared with three and a half days a Passover lamb stayed with a Jewish family) ministering mainly to the Israelites.

Therefore, if anyone accepts the atoning death of Yeshua on the cross for the remission of his sins, the blood of Yeshua will be applied on the lintel and the doorposts of his heart. When his life is over in this world, the death angel will pass over the door of his heart where the blood of the Lamb of God has been applied, and he will receive the gift of eternal life. Through the sacrificial death of the final Passover Lamb, the Scripture in Joel 2:32 has been fulfilled in Acts 2:21, *"And it shall come to pass that whoever calls on the name of the Lord shall be saved."*

After the death, resurrection, and ascension of Yeshua, the Messiah, and the coming of the Holy Spirit, now it is not only the Jews but also anyone who calls on the name of the Lord from all the Gentile families of the earth shall be saved. The salvation power of the blood of the final Passover Lamb has been flowing throughout the world for the past 2,000 years, and it will continue to flow until the day of the Second Coming of the Lord Yeshua in the near future.

Chapter 5

THE WAY THROUGH
THE WILDERNESS

God had decided to lead the Israelites around by way of the wilderness of the Red Sea to prevent them from returning to Egypt (Exodus 13:17-18). God demonstrated His divine love, mercy, grace, protection and power over the Israelites in order to transform them from their bondage of slave mentality (orphan spirit) to be the free children of the Creator God. He tested their hearts to see if they would obey His commandments, statutes, laws, judgments, and ways throughout their journey to the promise land. The Lord went before them by day in a pillar of cloud to lead the way and by night in a pillar of fire to give them light during their journey in the wilderness (Exodus 13:21-22).

Unfortunately, even after the Israelites had witnessed the great power, signs, wonders, and miracles of God during the course of their liberation in Egypt and throughout their journey with God in the wilderness, they continuously complained before God and His appointed servant Moses until the whole first generation of them, except Joshua and Caleb, completely perished. Their complaining began before they even crossed the Red Sea when they saw the Egyptian chariots drawing near them in Exodus 14:10-14:

*And when Pharaoh drew near, the children of Israel lifted their eyes, and behold, the Egyptians marched after them. So they were very afraid, and the children of Israel cried out to the Lord. Then they said to Moses, "Because there were no graves in Egypt, have you taken us away to die in the wilderness? Why have you so dealt with us, to bring us up out of Egypt?" Is this not the word that we told you in Egypt, saying, "Let us alone that we may serve the Egyptians? For it would have been better for us to serve the Egyptians than that we should die in the wilderness." And Moses said to the people, "**Do not be afraid. Stand still, and see the salvation of the Lord, which He will accomplish for you today.** For the Egyptians whom you see today, you shall see again no more forever. The Lord will fight for you, and you shall hold your peace."*

Since the Israelites had suffered under Egyptian bondage for 430 years, they did not know how to be free in the Lord and follow Him at all cost for the sake of freedom. Instead, they thought that it would have been better if they were in Egypt under Egyptian slavery. This poverty and slavery syndrome is also common among new followers of Yeshua, the Messiah. Once we come out of the bondage under Satan's control from our spiritual Egypt, we also must not look back or go back because of the challenges that we face in our new journey in the spiritual wilderness with the Lord. We must leave our comfort zone in the former spiritual Egypt where sins, bondage, and slavery dwell, and we must move forward with God into our new Promised Land by way of the wilderness where our faith and allegiance in Him will be challenged and tested. From that time on, the Israelites had to learn to trust the Lord, forget about the lifestyle of slavery in

Egypt, stand still and not be afraid of what dangers their physical eyes had observed around them, and witness the salvation of the Lord moving on behalf of them throughout their wandering in the wilderness. God was creating a special people group unto Himself. The Israelites had to learn to be a humble people through their own struggle of being slaves in Egypt. They had to be an obedient, faithful, loyal, disciplined, submissive, and holy people unto the Lord through their experience in the wilderness. At the same token, they had to be a courageous, bold, tenacious, determined, and persistent people through their conquering experience of going into the Promised Land.

THE RED SEA CROSSING

While the Egyptian army was chasing after the Israelites, who were camped in front of the Red Sea, the Lord commanded Moses to lift up his rod and stretch out his hand over the sea and divide it (Exodus 14:19-22):

And the Angel of God, who went before the camp of Israel, moved and went behind them; and the pillar of cloud went from before them and stood behind them. So it came between the camp of the Egyptians and the camp of Israel. Thus it was a cloud and darkness to the one, and it gave light by night to the other, so that the one did not come near the other all that night. Then Moses stretched out his hand over the sea; and the Lord caused the sea to go back by a strong east wind all that night, and made the sea into dry land, and the waters were divided. So the children of Israel went into the midst of the sea on the dry ground, and

*the waters were a wall to them on their right hand and
on their left.*

God allowed the Israelites to go through the midst of the
Red Sea on the dry ground while the waters formed a wall on
their right hand and on their left. However, the entire
Egyptian army that was chasing after the Israelites were all
drowned (Exodus 14:27-31). Therefore, God took them out of
the bondage of Egypt through the way that was humanly
impossible for them to go through and to return to Egypt, the
former way. God led them through His miraculous ways into
the wilderness so that no one could doubt His authority,
power, wisdom, presence, and lordship over created resources
(**Living Things**: The Lord turned the waters of Egypt into
blood in Exodus 7:19-20. He released the plagues of frogs,
lice, flies, livestock, locusts, and the firstborn over Egypt in
Exodus 8-11. **Nature**: The Lord released the plagues of boils,
hail, fire, and darkness before dividing the Red Sea in Exodus
9:8-10, 29; 14:21-31).

The crossing of the Red Sea is identified as a form of
baptism in 1 Corinthians 10:1-2: "*Moreover, brethren, I do
not want you to be unaware that all our fathers were under
the cloud, all passed through the sea, all were baptized into
Moses in the cloud and in the (Red) sea.*" One of the
meanings of "baptism" is "an act or experience by which one
is purified, sanctified, initiated, or named." In a way, only
after the Israelites went through the baptism of Moses were
they purified, sanctified, initiated, and named as God's chosen
people who were prepared to enter into the Promised Land to
become the nation called Israel. After the crossing of the Red
Sea, the Israelites were never allowed to look back or go back
to their old Egypt. However, the first generation of the
Israelites continuously sinned against God and perished in the

wilderness, because they were not totally set free from the slave mentality of Egypt.

I AM THE LORD WHO HEALS YOU

Once the Israelites came into the wilderness, they began to complain against Moses, saying, *"What shall we drink?"* Of course, they were only concerned about the physical source of water to survive in the wilderness. However, God was not only interested in providing their physical need of water but also their absolute necessity of spiritual water (the living water from the Rock). Therefore, God began to provide them with His ordinances, laws, commandments, and statutes to live by as His special people group on the face of the earth. The first ordinance that God declared to them was written in Exodus 15:26, *"If you **diligently heed the voice of the Lord** your God and **do what is right in His sight, give ear to His commandments and keep all His statutes**, I will put none of the diseases on you which I have brought on the Egyptians. **For I am the Lord who heals you.**"*

The first provision of God's spiritual water for the Israelites was to provide the conditions for them to receive His divine health. They received abundant blessings of gold, silver, flocks, fame, and the land with milk and honey flowing. However, if they did not have God's divine health to enjoy His provisions, then this would not amount to much for the Israelites as the real blessings. Even in this twenty-first century, people spend enormous amounts of money to preserve their health apart from following God's ordinances. When some believers of God become sick, they often claim God's healing Scriptures and rebuke different kinds of spirit of infirmities to receive their healing, without fully obeying the commandments of God. But according to Exodus 15:26, we need to follow God's simple four steps of instructions to receive His divine healing in our lives:

Diligently heed the voice of the Lord your God: In order for you to hear the voice of the Lord your God, you need to spend much time in prayer talking and listening to Him in accordance with Jeremiah 29:11-13, *"For I know the thoughts that I think toward you, says the Lord, thoughts of peace and not of evil, to give you a future and a hope. Then you will call upon Me and go and pray to Me, and I will listen to you. And you will seek Me and find Me, when you search for Me with all your heart."*

Do what is right in His sight: Once you know the voice of the Lord for your life, you need to do what is right not in your sight but in His sight. God knows and sees all that you think and do. It is easy to give lip service to Him, but it takes commitment in your heart to do what is right in His sight. The word of God speaks about the heroes of the Bible as the ones who did what was right in the sight of the Lord:

"Then it shall be, if you heed all that I command you, walk in My ways, and do what is right in My sight, to keep My statutes and My commandments, as My servant David did..." (1 King 11:38a)
"Joash did what was right in the sight of the Lord all the days of Jehoiada the priest." (2 Chronicles 24:2)
"And he (Uzziah) did what was right in the sight of the Lord, according to all that his father Amaziah had done." (2 Chronicles 26:4)

Give ear to His commandments: The meaning of "commandment" is the act or power of commanding or something that is commanded. This means the commandments of God are not just suggestions for you to keep whenever you agree with them or you feel like following them according to your own convenience. But, they are His divine rules that we must abide by in order to reap His blessings and avoid curses. The Lord established the conditional blessings in Deuteronomy 28:1, "*Now it shall come to pass, if you diligently obey the voice of the Lord your God, to observe carefully all His commandments which I command you today, that the Lord your God will set you high above all nations of the earth.*"

Keep all His statutes: *Nelson's Illustrated Bible Dictionary* states the meaning of "statute" as "a decree or law issued by a ruler or governing body, or especially by God as the Supreme Ruler." If you break His statutes (decrees or laws), then you must expect to receive the consequence or penalty of breaking His laws just like when you break the traffic laws and are caught by a policeman. You want to obey His statutes so that you can be praised by the Lord just like Abraham was praised in Genesis 26:4-5, "*And I will make your descendants multiply as the stars of heaven; I will give to your descendants all these lands; and in your seed all the nations of the earth shall be blessed; because Abraham obeyed My voice and kept My charges, My commandments, My statutes, and My laws.*"

The foundation of receiving God's divine protection over any attacks of the evil force of darkness is to obey His commandments, judgments, laws, and statutes with the fear of the Him in our heart. If God's favor is upon you, no weapon formed against you shall prosper. You will be set apart as a chosen generation, a royal priesthood, a holy nation, His own special people, that you may proclaim the praises of Him who called you out of darkness into His marvelous light (2 Peter 2:9).

BREAD FROM HEAVEN

Once again, the Israelites complained before God saying, *"Oh, that we had died by the hand of the Lord in the land of Egypt, when we sat by the pots of meat and when we ate bread to the full! For you have brought us out into this wilderness to kill this whole assembly with hunger"* (Exodus 16:3). In response to their complaints, the Lord said to Moses in Exodus 16:4, *"Behold, I will rain bread from heaven for you. And the people shall go out and gather a certain quota every day, that I may test them, whether they will walk in My law or not."* They were very impatient and did not trust the Lord with all their heart. If God calls you, He will provide you with all of your needs to fulfill His purpose and plan in your life. Once you are walking into the direction where God has called you to go, then one of the most important things that you must do is to totally trust Him for your provisions.

The wilderness is the place where God will test your faith, commitment, loyalty, trustworthiness, motive, integrity, and intent of your heart. While you are in your own wilderness, the Lord will only provide exactly what you need and not more. His provision for you will not come when you want it but usually at the very last minute to test your heart. In many cases, He will not even allow you to sustain yourself by utilizing your own skills and old ways of acquiring means. But you have to wait upon the Lord to send His divine bread from heaven to provide for you. You may have to depend on other people's support to initiate, sustain, and move forward with His plan in your life. In order to receive the bread from heaven for your survival, you have to humble yourself before God and men without complaining about your lack or want. As long as the Israelites were in the wilderness, they ate manna (the bread of heaven that they called *"What is it?"* in Hebrew) for forty years until they came to the border of the land of Canaan (Exodus 16:35).

In the New Testament, Yeshua said in John 6:48 & 51a, *"I am the bread of life. I am the living bread which came down from heaven. If anyone eats of this bread, he will live forever..."* Thus, Yeshua, the Messiah, is the Manna from heaven to provide us with the eternal Bread of Life. As we journey through our own wilderness of this life, we must depend on the Bread of Life and not the bread of this world for our sustenance each day. Just like the Israelites ate manna in order to receive life in the wilderness, we can receive abundant life on earth and eternal life in heaven as we receive the Bread of Life, Yeshua the Messiah. Thus, the believers of Yeshua have been partaking the Communion or the Lord's Supper in that we actually eat a broken piece of the Communion bread, the symbol of the broken body of the Messiah.

WATER FROM THE ROCK

Again, as the Israelites journeyed into the wilderness, they began to contend with Moses in Exodus 17:3b, *"Why is it you have brought us up out of Egypt, to kill us and our children and our livestock with thirst?"* The Lord responded to Moses' intercession for the people in Exodus 17:6, *"Behold, I will stand before you there on the rock in Horeb; and you shall strike the rock, and water will come out of it, that the people may drink.*" Horeb was called the mountain of God (Exodus 3:1) where Moses heard God speaking through the burning bush and where the law was given to Israel. In the wilderness, drinkable water was one of the most important survival elements. Without water, the Israelites were not able to survive. Since they had witnessed numerous signs, wonders, and miracles of the Lord throughout their journey, they should have trusted Him for the supply of water as well. If they had put their faith in God and cried out to Him for the provision of water, He would have been very glad to provide all their needs.

However, they began to complain before Moses and God for their lack once again. Naturally speaking, it is impossible for a rock to pour out water for approximately two million Israelites in the wilderness, but God led them to the rock in the mountain Horeb to provide His supernatural source of water for them. In the Bible, "Rock" is one of the symbols to identify God or the Messiah (the Christ): "*For who is God, except the Lord? And who is a **rock**, except our God?*" (2 Samuel 22:32). "*The Lord lives! Blessed be my **Rock**! Let God be exalted, the **Rock** of my salvation!*" (2 Samuel 22:47). "*The Lord is my **Rock** and my fortress and my deliverer; my God, my strength, in whom I will trust*" (Psalm 18:2). "*Because you have forgotten the God of your salvation, and have not been mindful of the **Rock** of your stronghold*" (Isaiah 17:10). "*...on this **rock*** (Peter's confession in Matthew 16:16, '*You are the Christ, the Son of the living God.*') *I will build My church, and the gates of Hades shall not prevail against it*" (Matthew 16:18). "*For they drank of that spiritual **Rock** that followed them, and that **Rock** was Christ (Messiah)*" (1 Corinthians 10:4). Figuratively speaking, "water" in the Bible is identified as one of the symbols of God, the Holy Spirit:

*"Therefore with joy you will draw **water** from the wells of salvation"* (Isaiah 12:3). *"Ho! Everyone who thirsts, come to the **waters**; and you who have no money, come, buy and eat"* (Isaiah 55:1). *"But the **water** that I shall give him will become in him a fountain of **water** springing up into everlasting life"* (John 4:14b). *"He who believes in Me (Yeshua or Jesus the Messiah), as the Scripture has said, out of his heart will flow **rivers of living water**. But this He spoke concerning the Spirit, whom those believing in Him would receive"* (John 7:38-39). *"And he showed me a pure **river of water of life**"* (Revelation 22:1). *"Come! And let him who thirsts come. Whoever desires, let him take **the water of life** freely"* (Revelation 22:17b).

Therefore, when God allowed the water to come out of the rock, He was figuratively demonstrating that the Rock (Messiah) would come in the future to save not only the Jews but also the Gentiles of the world. Whosoever would believe in Yeshua, the Messiah, (Jesus Christ, the Rock) would receive the Living Water, God the Holy Spirit, who would seal the believers as the guarantee of the heavenly inheritance (Ephesians 1:13-14).

THE TEN COMMANDMENTS

After God miraculously provided the basic sustenance for the Israelites so that they might totally depend on Him for their daily needs in the wilderness, He established the spiritual law for them to follow. These laws of God would separate them from the practices of other pagan people groups in the region. In order for God to separate the Israelites as His chosen people group and to release His divine blessings upon them, they had to abide by His laws, commandments, statutes, and judgments. God's intention for the Israelites had been revealed very clearly in Deuteronomy 30:15-20:

> *See, I have set before you today **life and good, death
> and evil**, in that I command you today to love the Lord
> your God, **to walk in His ways, and to keep His
> commandments, His statutes, and His judgments**,
> that you may live and multiply; and the Lord your God
> will bless you in the land which you go to possess. But
> if your heart turns away so that you do not hear, and
> are drawn away, and worship other gods and serve
> them, I announce to you today that you shall surely
> perish; you shall not prolong your days in the land
> which you cross over the Jordan to go in and possess.
> I call heaven and earth as witnesses today against
> you, that **I have set before you life and death,
> blessing and cursing; therefore choose life**, that both
> you and your descendants may live; that you may love
> the Lord your God, that you may obey His voice, and
> that you may cling to Him, for He is your life and the
> length of your days; and that you may dwell in the
> land which the Lord swore to your fathers, to
> Abraham, Isaac, and Jacob, to give them.*

In the Garden of Eden, God's Paradise on the earth, the
Lord only gave one commandment for Adam and Eve to live
by. However, they could not obey even one law of God in
Genesis 2:16-17, and they were kicked out of Paradise into
the cursed world where Satan was the ruler. All nations,
tribes, peoples, and tongues were worshipping idols, demons,
false religions and gods influenced by the lies of the devil. In
order for God to preserve the Israelites from the influence of
Satan in this cursed world, He had to establish the
foundational law with them—the Ten Commandments in
Exodus 20:1-17:

1) *You shall have no other gods before Me*: The first and foremost commandment was for the Israelites to follow the one and only Living God (Yahweh) who created heaven and earth and all that is in them.

2) *You shall not make for yourself a carved image,* and you shall not bow down to them nor serve them: God strictly warned the Israelites not to make any idols to worship, as the pagans had done.

3) *You shall not take the name of the Lord your God in vain*: The Creator God demanded the utmost respect of His name from the Israelites. Respecting His name means to honor and fear the Almighty God and His divine power, authority, laws, commandments, statutes, judgments, attributes, character, love, mercy, and grace.

4) *Remember the Sabbath day to keep it holy*: God commanded the Israelites, *"Six days you shall labor and do all your work, but the seventh day is the Sabbath of the Lord your God. In it you shall do no work."* God created the universe in six days and rested on the seventh in Genesis 1; therefore, the practice of Sabbath day began from the time of Creation. It was God's law that men would observe one day out of a week to rest and worship Him.

The keeping of the Sabbath was a sign that the Israelites truly accepted His Lordship over them. To break His Sabbatical law was to rebel against Him and would bring the death penalty (Exodus 31:12-18). However, in the New Testament, Yeshua, the Messiah, declared that He was the Lord of the Sabbath (Mark 2:28), as He went about healing the sick and casting out demons on the Sabbath. He also defined the purpose of Sabbath in Mark 2:27: *"The Sabbath was made for man, and not man for the Sabbath."*

5) *Honor your father and your mother*: God also established a specific commandment for children to honor their father and mother. The result of honoring one's parents would bring God's divine benefit to children, according to Exodus 20:12, *"Your days may be long upon the land which the Lord your God is giving you."* This same commandment was reiterated in Ephesians 6:2-3, *"Honor your father and mother, which is the first commandment with promise: that it may be well with you and you may live long on the earth."* Dishonoring one's parents could result in shortening the days of the child's life in the land.

6) *You shall not murder*: "Murder" means "the crime of unlawfully killing a person with malice aforethought." According to Genesis 1:26-27, man is created in God's image and likeness, so murdering a human being is a serious crime before God and must be punished based on Genesis 9:6, *"Whoever sheds man's blood, by man his blood shall be shed; for in the image of God He made man."* Only the Creator God has the power over anyone's life and death as stated in 1 Samuel 2:6, *"The Lord kills and makes alive; He brings down to the grave and brings up."*

In accordance with God's word to the Prophet Jeremiah, a human life begins in the womb: *"Before I formed you in the womb I knew you; before you were born I sanctified you; I ordained you a prophet to the nations"* (Jeremiah 1:5). Also God reaffirms His formation of life beginning in the womb in Isaiah 49:1 and 5, *"The Lord has called me from the womb; from the matrix of my mother He has made mention of my name. And now the Lord says, who formed me from the womb to be His Servant."*

If God knew us before we were ever even formed in our mothers' womb, then all life truly begins with Him and is a gift from Him. Therefore, aborting a baby in a mother's womb is murdering a gift of life from God, regardless of the circumstance how the baby might have been formed. Other facets of this commandment include not only abortion, but also the termination of developmentally disabled or genetically defected fetuses or babies. After all, before ultrasound technology existed, pregnant women were not able to test for these deformities and did not have an option to abort their babies on the grounds of deformities. By the same token, mercy killings and assisted suicides of terminally ill patients (euthanasia) are also considered the murder of human beings. Life comes from God, and He alone has the right to terminate any human life. However, God authorized capital punishment in the Old Testament for anyone who disobeys His certain specific laws as in Exodus 21:14-17:

But if a man acts with premeditation against his neighbor, to kill him by treachery, you shall take him from My altar, that he may die. And he who strikes his father or his mother shall surely be put to death. He who kidnaps a man and sells him, or if he is found in his hand, shall surely be put to death. And he who curses his father or his mother shall surely be put to death.

Again, the Creator God has the absolute right to establish His law to save or take away human life, but a created human being is not allowed to terminate any life. However, if you are a member of a legitimate military force of a recognized government and your country has been invaded by an enemy force, you are called to defend your country. When Lot was taken by the king of Shinar, king of Ellasar, king of Elam and Tidal king of nations, Abram armed his three hundred and eighteen trained servants who were born in his own house, and went in pursuit as far as Dan, and he brought back his brother Lot and his goods, as well as the women and the people (Genesis 14:1-16).

7) *You shall not commit adultery*: An act of adultery will destroy the fabric of a God-ordained marriage as well as the families involved. In the Old Testament days, the punishment for adultery was a death penalty found in Leviticus 20:10, *"The man who commits adultery with another man's wife, he who commits adultery with his neighbor's wife, the adulterer and the adulteress, shall surely be put to death."* However, in the New Testament, Yeshua redefined the act of adultery in Matthew 5:28 and 32, *"But I say to you that whoever looks at a woman to lust for her has already committed adultery with her in his heart. But I say to you that whoever divorces his wife for any reason except sexual immorality causes her to commit adultery; and whoever marries a woman who is divorced commits adultery."*

However, God demonstrated His grace and mercy to King David in the Old Testament when he committed the sin of adultery with Bathsheba and murdered her husband, Uriah, because he sincerely repented of his sin before God. Nevertheless, the consequence of King David's sin followed him. One disaster after another struck his family, including rape, murder, and revolt (2 Samuel 13-15). In the New Testament, Yeshua forgave a woman who was caught in the act of adultery in John 8:7b; 10-11, *"He who is without sin among you, let him throw a stone at her first... 'Woman, where are those accusers of yours? Has no one condemned you?' 'Neither do I condemn you; go and sin no more.'"* God's divine forgiveness, even for the sin of adultery, is not to condone the sin but to lead us from darkness back to His light as in John 8:12, *"I am the light of the world. He who follows Me shall not walk in darkness, but have the light of life."*

8) *You shall not steal*: It is very obvious that one must not take possession of anything belonging to someone else without his or her permission. God made a law against stealing in Exodus 22:1, *"If a man steals an ox or a sheep, and slaughters it or sells it, he shall restore five oxen for an* *ox and four sheep for a sheep."* Therefore, if you have stolen anything from anyone, you need to restore four to five times of what you have taken. Also, false reporting on income tax is a form of stealing from the government (Matthew 22:15-21). Furthermore, we must not rob God by not giving our full tithes and offerings. According to Malachi 3:8-11 and Matthew 23:23, Jesus said, *"You should tithe, yes, but do not neglect the more important things."* Therefore, God's commandment to tithe is not only the Old Testament ordinance but also the New Testament's as well.

9) *You shall not bear false witness against your neighbor*: A false witness or report against anyone can truly ruin one's reputation, integrity, and trustworthiness. Therefore God also warns against it in Exodus 23:1-3, *"You shall not circulate a false report. Do not put your hand with the wicked to be an unrighteous witness. You shall not follow a crowd to do evil; nor shall you testify in a dispute so as to turn aside after many to pervert justice. You shall not show partiality to a poor man in his dispute."*

10) *You shall not covet*: To covet is to feel an inordinate desire for what belongs to another. A covetous heart will desire what ones neighbors have, even though it is beyond the limit of your means. In the Old Testament, when Lot was separated from Abraham, he coveted after the plain of Jordan toward Sodom and Gomorrah (Genesis 13:10-11). Eventually, Lot lost everything that he coveted after in Sodom and Gomorrah when God destroyed them with brimstone and fire (Genesis 19:12-29).

In the New Testament, Judas Iscariot coveted after thirty pieces of silver, betraying Yeshua, the Messiah (Matthew 26:14-16). Eventually, he became remorseful and hanged himself (Matthew 27:3-5). Besides the Ten Commandments (the moral laws), God also provided the civil laws (Exodus 31:12-18) and the ceremonial laws (Leviticus 23) for the

Israelites in the wilderness. God established these laws for them so they would first obey His commandments solely: trusting and worshiping Him—the one and only Living God, and to create and maintain order in the community through the civil and moral laws.

THE TABERNACLE

God commanded Moses to build the Tabernacle where He could dwell with the Israelites in the wilderness. In this Tabernacle, there were no other man-made idols for the Israelites to worship, but the presence of God rested on the Ark of the Covenant inside the Most Holy place. The Ark contained the golden pot that held the manna, Aaron's rod that budded, and the tablets of the covenant. These three symbolic objects were the Old Testament typology of Yeshua, the Messiah (Jesus Christ):

The manna: While the Israelites were traveling through the wilderness, God provided His special food, manna (bread from heaven), for them to eat for forty years according to Exodus 16:10-15, 35:

> *Now it came to pass, as Aaron spoke to the whole congregation of the children of Israel, that they looked toward the wilderness, and behold, the glory of the Lord appeared in the cloud. And the Lord spoke to Moses, saying, "I have heard the complaints of the children of Israel. Speak to them, saying, 'At twilight you shall eat meat, and in the morning you shall be filled with bread. And you shall know that I am the Lord your God.'" So it was that quails came up at*

*evening and covered the camp, and in the morning the dew lay all around the camp. And when the layer of dew lifted, there on the surface of the wilderness, was a small round substance, as fine as frost on the ground. So when the children of Israel saw it, they said to one another, "**What is it (in Hebrew: manna)?**" For they did not know what it was. And Moses said to them, "This is the bread which the Lord has given you to eat* (vss. 10-15)." *And the children of Israel ate manna forty years, until they came to an inhabited land; they ate manna until they came to the border of the land of Canaan* (vs. 35).

God's manna stopped when they began to eat the produce of the Promise land according to Joshua 5:12, "*Then the manna ceased on the day after they had eaten the produce of the land; and the children of Israel no longer had manna, but they ate the food of the land of Canaan that year.*" However in the New Testament, Yeshua declares that He is the bread of life who comes from heaven in John 6:32-33; 35, "*Moses did not give you the bread from heaven, but My Father gives you the true bread from heaven. For the bread of God is He who comes down from heaven and gives life to the world... I am the bread of life. He who comes to Me shall never hunger, and he who believes in Me shall never thirst.*" **Therefore, Yeshua is the fulfillment of the true bread from heaven to provide the bread of life to whosoever calls upon His name from every people, tribe, tongue and nation.**

***Aaron's Rod*—Aaron's rod that budded symbolizes the resurrection:** "*The rod of Aaron, of the house of Levi, had sprouted and put forth buds, had produced blossoms and yielded ripe almonds*" (Numbers 17:8b). The dead rod of Aaron produced life and sprouted. Likewise, anyone who puts his total trust in Yeshua, the Messiah, and takes hold of the Eternal Rod of God will also experience new fruit, life, and resurrection in his life. Thus, Yeshua declared in John 11:25, *"I am the resurrection and the life."* The Son of the Living God who arose from the grave to conquer sin, sickness, curses, fear of death, and Satan can provide His divine resurrection and life to anyone who believes in Him.

The Tablets of the Covenant (Ten Commandments): The Ten Commandments were given to the Israelites to abide by God's laws and commandments all the days of their lives in this world. Yeshua came to fulfill the law as described in Matthew 5:17: *"Do not think that I came to destroy the Law or the Prophets. I did not come to destroy but to fulfill."* He came not only to fulfill the Law but also to establish the New Covenant in accordance with Jeremiah 31:31; 33b, *"Behold, the days are coming, says the Lord, when **I will make a new covenant with the house of Israel** and with the house of Judah...I will put My law in their minds, and write it on their hearts; and I will be their God, and they shall be My people."*

The New Covenant through Yeshua, the Messiah, is for the house of Israel as well as for all the families of the earth who will call upon His name as their Lord and Savior. The Old Covenant was solely given to the Israelites in order to prepare the way for all the families of the earth to find the way of salvation through the New Covenant in God's only Son, Yeshua, the Messiah, Son of Abraham and Son of David.

The New Covenant is the fulfillment of the Old Covenant of Genesis 12:1-3 (Fulfilled in Galatians 3:8) and 2 Samuel 7:16 (Fulfilled in Luke 1:32-33) through Yeshua, the Lamb and the Lion of God, to bring the salvation and kingdom plans to the lost humanity. As Yeshua dwells in the heart of a New Covenant believer of God, his heart symbolically becomes the most holy place where the New Ark of the Covenant (Yeshua, the Messiah) exists. Thus, His presence in a believer's life allows Him to write God's law in his mind and heart to fulfill the law and the prophets. When Moses finished the work in Exodus 40:34, the glory of the Lord filled the Tabernacle. The Tabernacle without the glory of the Lord is nothing but a man-made building. As the glory of the Lord filled the Tabernacle, it became the place where God, once again, dwelt with His chosen people. In the New Covenant, the glory of God fills human temples from all nations, tribes, peoples and tongues (Revelation 7:9), with the Holy Spirit as they become believers of Yeshua, the Lamb of God.

Therefore, the Old Testament Tabernacle and Temple of God were only given for the Israelites as the witness to the surrounding nations that the Creator God indwelled with His chosen people in Jerusalem. While the Old Covenant was primarily available for the Jews, the New Covenant, created through the death and resurrection of the Son of Abraham and the Son of David, is accessible to anyone who calls upon the Name above all names, Yeshua the Messiah.

MOSES AND JOSHUA

Moses brought the Law of God to the Israelites so they might abide by God's law and receive His divine blessings, according to Deuteronomy 28:1-14. However, the rebellious first generation of Israelites sinned before God in the wilderness for forty years. Except for Joshua and Caleb, the rest of the Israelites perished, including Moses and Aaron. It was Joshua (whose name is another form of Yeshua and means "Yahweh is salvation") who led the Israelites into the Promised Land. Moses symbolizes the Old Testament law and Old Covenant. Trying to abide by the Mosaic Law alone, like the Pharisees in the New Testament era did, is not enough for one to receive God's pardon for one's sin and to enter into His spiritual kingdom on earth and the eternal Promised Land in heaven after death. In the Old Testament, Joshua (meaning "Yahweh is salvation") was appointed by God after the death of Moses to lead the Israelites into the Promise Land. In the New Testament, the new Joshua, Yeshua (meaning "the Lord, Yahweh who is salvation") as the final Lamb of God had to die on the Cross for the sins of the world to provide the way, the truth, and the life to His chosen people (those who believe in Yeshua), so that they can enter into the eternal Promised Land. God's New Covenant with His chosen people, according to Jeremiah 31:31-34, was actualized through Yeshua as the Mediator. God declared in verse 33b, *"I will put My law in their minds, and write it on their hearts; and I will be their God, and they shall be My people."* Yeshua was the last sacrificial Lamb of the Old Covenant and is the Mediator of the New Covenant (Hebrews 9:12-15):

> *Not with the blood of goats and calves, but with His own blood He entered the Most Holy Place once for all, having obtained eternal redemption.* For if the blood of bulls and goats and the ashes of a heifer, sprinkling the unclean, sanctifies for the purifying of the flesh, *how much more shall the blood of Christ, who through the eternal Spirit offered Himself without spot to God, purge your conscience from dead works to serve the living God?* And for this reason *He is the Mediator of the new covenant,* by means of death, for the redemption of the transgressions under the first covenant, that *those who are called may receive the promise of the eternal inheritance.*

Again in Matthew 17:1-5, Moses came down to talk with Yeshua, the New Joshua, in the place where Jesus was transfigured:

*And after six days Jesus took Peter, James, and John his brother, led them up on a high mountain by themselves; and He was transfigured before them. His face shone like the sun, and His clothes became as white as the light. And behold, **Moses and Elijah appeared to them**, talking with Him. Then Peter answered and said to Jesus, "Lord, it is good for us to be here; if You wish, let us make here three tabernacles: one for You, one for Moses, and one for Elijah." While he was still speaking, behold, a bright cloud overshadowed them; and suddenly a voice came out of the cloud, saying, "This is My beloved Son, in whom I am well pleased. Hear Him!"*

Could it be possible that Moses passed the baton of the Old Covenant to the New Joshua in order to initiate the New Covenant to conquer the spiritual Promised Land in Israel as well as in the nations of the world? The Father God also spoke in Matthew 17:5b, ***"This is My beloved Son, in whom I am well pleased. Hear Him!"***

No other person than the Father God (Yahweh) the Creator of the Universe, the God of the Old Covenant was speaking to the New Covenant people including the Jews. *"Hear Him, the messages of Yeshua the Messiah* (Jesus Christ)." It is time to hear the voice of the Son of the Living God who initiated the New Covenant with His own blood on the cross as the final Lamb of God.

Chapter 6

THE DAVIDIC COVENANT
(The Kingdom Plan)

⁓⁓⁓

God's deliverance plan was continuously at work through King David. In 2 Samuel 7:16, God promised King David that his house and his kingdom would be established forever. However, before the end of the Old Testament era, David's kingdom was divided into Israel and Judah, and they were eventually annexed by the different kingdoms of the Babylonians, Assyrians, Persians, Greeks, Egyptians, and the Roman Empire. Therefore, God's covenant with King David was not fulfilled through the physical kingdom of David. Thus, we need to examine the spiritual implication of God's covenant with King David in 2 Samuel 7:16, *"And your house and your kingdom shall be established forever before you. Your throne shall be established forever."*

God was once again reestablishing His eternal kingdom on earth with His chosen people, who would obey and abide by His kingdom principles and rules. God's divine plan was to expand His kingdom plan to affect all the families of the earth. It was His divine plan to establish the eternal King of Kings who would sit on the throne of David to rule the world with His love, grace, mercy, power, authority, dominion, and righteous judgment. In order for the Messiah to be the One who would provide the perfect salvation plan and the kingdom plan for the Jews and for all the Gentiles of the world, He had to fulfill the Old Covenant as well as the New Covenant of God in His life.

In order for God to provide the perfect salvation plan for all mankind, He had to send the sinless Son of God to become the sinless Son of Man. Any sinful man cannot atone and pay for the sins of another fallen human being. Therefore, Yeshua had to die on the cross as the final Lamb of God to fulfill the Old Covenant requirements. He arose from the dead not as the resurrected Lamb, but as the Lion of Judah, to sit on the throne of the King David as the King of Kings and the Lord of Lords, fulfilling the New Covenant and preparing the way to expand the kingdom of God throughout the world. The Messiah's birth and His kingship over the throne of David were prophesied in Isaiah 9:7 and in Luke 1:32-33:

*Of the increase of His government and peace there will be no end, **upon the throne of David and over His kingdom**, to order it and establish it with judgment and justice from that time forward, even forever.* (Isaiah 9:7)

*He will be great, and will be called the Son of the Highest; **and the Lord God will give Him the throne of His father David**. And He will reign over the house of Jacob forever, and of His kingdom there will be no end.* (Luke 1:32-33)

God's divine **salvation plan** is characterized through the Passover ceremony by sacrificing a lamb for the atonement of sin. Through the establishment of God's eternal kingdom with King David and His chosen people, God was reestablishing His **kingdom plan** on earth. Whosoever will accept God's divine salvation plan will receive the right to be God's kingdom citizen through His kingdom plan. Anyone who is outside of God's kingdom is bound by the power of the kingdom of darkness. However, once you are born again into the kingdom of God through Yeshua the Messiah, the Mediator between God and man, you will become a son or daughter of the King of Kings and the Lord of Lords. During the Old Testament days, God established the physical kingdom of Israel to demonstrate His power, lordship, authority, wisdom, grace, mercy, and judgment over not only the Israelites but also the surrounding Gentile nations.

The kingdom of Israel had the kings Saul, David, and Solomon who had been handpicked and anointed by the Lord through His chosen prophets before the division of the kingdom. These kings knew that the King of Kings and the Lord of Lords, the Creator God, Yahweh appointed them. The Lord dwelled with His chosen people. God's presence and glory rested on the mercy seat of the Ark of the Covenant inside the most holy place in the Temple.

Therefore, the kingdom of Israel was God's extension of His kingdom of heaven on earth. God's kingdom invaded into the kingdom of Satan on earth to destroy and demolish his wicked rule over the fallen humanity. During the Old Covenant, God's manifestation of His kingdom authority, power, rule, and plan were directly connected to the physical kingdom of the Israelites as His divine tool to shine His glory to the nations.

However, in the New Covenant, God's kingdom plan is not only for the Israelites but also for all the families of the earth—to invade into every nation, people, tongue, and tribe. So God sent the King of Kings and the Lord of Lords, Yeshua, as **the Messiah not only for the Jews but also for the Gentiles to initiate the kingdom plan on earth**. The first preaching of Yeshua in Matthew 4:17 confirms, *"Repent, for*

the kingdom of heaven *is at hand*." He also taught us to preach the kingdom of heaven in Matthew 10:7-8.

DANIEL'S VISION OF THE COMING KINGDOM OF GOD

The prophet Daniel also prophesied the coming kingdom of God throughout the book of Daniel. The first prophecy was given when Daniel interpreted King Nebuchadnezzar's dream in Daniel 2:32-35:

This image's head was of fine gold, its chest and arms of silver, its belly and thighs of bronze, its legs of iron, its feet partly of iron and partly of clay. You watched while a stone was cut out without hands, which struck the image on its feet of iron and clay, and broke them in pieces. Then the iron, the clay, the bronze, the silver, and the gold were crushed together, and became like chaff from the summer threshing floors; the wind carried them away so that no trace of them was found. **And the stone that struck the image became a great mountain and filled the whole earth.**

Daniel prophesied that there would arise three other kingdoms that would be inferior to the Babylonian kingdom. But he prophesied that ultimately the stone (the kingdom of God) would strike the image (the symbols of four kingdoms or kingdoms of the world). It would become like chaff with the wind carrying these kingdoms away without trace. Eventually the kingdom of God would become a great mountain and fill the whole earth.

Daniel further prophesied about the kingdom that the God of heaven would establish in chapter 2:44-45:

*And in the days of these kings **the God of heaven will set up a kingdom which shall never be destroyed;** and the kingdom shall not be left to other people; it shall break in pieces and consume all these kingdoms, and it shall stand forever. Inasmuch as you saw that the stone was cut out of the mountain without hands, and that it broke in pieces the iron, the bronze, the clay, the silver, and the gold—the great God has made known to the king what will come to pass after this. The dream is certain, and its interpretation is sure.*

It is very clear that the God of heaven will establish the kingdom of heaven on earth and it shall eventually destroy and consume all other kingdoms of the world; however, the kingdom of heaven shall never be destroyed. What God will establish on earth will never be altered, subjugated, or destroyed by any other kingdoms of the world. Again, Daniel prophesied the coming of the Messiah and His kingdom in Daniel 7:13-14:

*And behold, **One like the Son of Man, Coming with the clouds of heaven!** He came to the Ancient of Days, and they brought Him near before Him. **Then to Him was given dominion and glory and a kingdom, that all peoples, nations, and languages should serve Him.** His dominion is an everlasting dominion, which shall not pass away, and His kingdom the one which shall not be destroyed.*

According to Daniel's prophecy, the Son of Man would come to receive dominion, glory, and a kingdom over all peoples, nations, and languages in the world. His kingdom and dominion shall not be destroyed. Daniel further prophesied that the kingdom of God would be given to the saints of the Most High in Daniel 7:18, 21-22, 27:

> *But the saints of the Most High shall receive the kingdom, and possess the kingdom forever, even forever and ever* (Daniel 7:18). *I was watching; and the same horn was making war against the saints, and prevailing against them, until the Ancient of Days came, and a judgment was made in favor of the saints of the Most High, and the time came for the saints to possess the kingdom* (Daniel 7:21-22). *Then the kingdom and dominion, and the greatness of the kingdoms under the whole heaven, shall be given to the people, the saints of the Most High. His kingdom is an everlasting kingdom, and all dominions shall serve and obey Him* (Daniel 7:27).

Once the Son of Man, Yeshua the Messiah, firmly established the kingdom of God on the earth, He would release it to the saints of the Most High, and they would possess it forever and ever. However, Daniel was not talking about the physical kingdom of God but the spiritual one to fulfill the prophecies in Genesis 3:15 and 12:3. The first order was for the Son of Man to come as the last Adam—to die on the cross as the final Lamb of God so He could take away the sins of the world and to crucify our old man with Him on the cross so that the body of sin might be done away with (Romans 6:3-6).

Under the power of the first Adam's DNA, all mankind have to die, but once we are in Christ (in the last Adam's DNA), all the blessings of Christ become ours to enjoy—abundant life on the earth and eternal life in heaven. We can claim Romans 8:1-2, *"There is therefore now no condemnation to those who are in Christ Jesus, who do not walk according to the flesh, but according to the Spirit. For the law of the Spirit of life in Christ Jesus has made me free from the law of sin and death."* If we are in (inside of) Christ (John 14:20), then we will walk according to the Spirit because He always walks in the Spirit. But if we are controlled by the first Adam's DNA, then there will be much condemnation because we will be under the original curses of the fallen man.

When He arose from the grave, He became the Lion of Judah who crushed the head of the devil, according to Genesis 3:15. He took away the usurped authority of Satan over the kingdoms of the world and established the spiritual kingdom of heaven on earth as He sat on the throne of David as the King of Kings and the Lord of Lords. God's salvation plan opened the door not only for the Jews but also for all the families of the earth according to His promise in Genesis 12:3. Those who became sons and daughters of God through accepting the perfect salvation plan of God in Yeshua (John 1:12) became the saints of the Most High God to inherit and possess the kingdom of heaven on the earth.

After Yeshua ascended to heaven, He sent the Holy Spirit to rest upon a hundred and twenty believers on the day of Pentecost, ushering in the spiritual kingdom of God on the earth. Through the presence of the Holy Spirit upon the saints, these believers were able to possess the kingdom of God as His chosen children or Christians (little Christ or Anointed One) to do the works of Yeshua, the Messiah (Jesus Christ), on the earth according to the promise in John 14:12, *"Most assuredly, I say to you, he who believes in Me, the works that I do he will do also; and greater works than these he will do, because I go to My Father."*

GOD'S TEMPLE

When King Solomon finished building God's Temple and had set up the Ark of the Covenant into the Most Holy Place, the glory of the Lord filled the house of the Lord in 1 Kings 8:10-11. Without the presence and glory of God, God's Temple is nothing but a man-made building. God's presence separates and distinguishes His Temple from Buddhist, Hindu, Muslim, Mormon, Jehovah's Witness, and any other man-made temples where idols, religious doctrines, and objects are worshipped. As the glory of the Lord filled the Temple, it became the place where God dwelt with His chosen people on the earth. The most important place inside the Temple was the Most Holy Place where the Ark of the Covenant was placed. God commanded Moses to put the mercy seat on top of the Ark where He would meet Moses in Exodus 25:21-22:

You shall put the mercy seat on top of the ark, and in the ark you shall put the Testimony that I will give you. And there I will meet with you, and I will speak with you from above the mercy seat, from between the two cherubim which are on the ark of the Testimony, of all things which I will give you in commandment to the children of Israel.

God exercised His mercy, grace, and forgiveness of sin over the Israelites from above **the mercy seat** in the Most Holy Place. The high priest annually sprinkled the blood of sacrificial animals on the mercy seat during its appointed time in accordance with Leviticus 16:15-16, 30 to receive His mercy and forgiveness for the sins of the Israelites:

Then he shall kill the goat of the sin offering, which is for the people, bring its blood inside the veil, do with that blood as he did with the blood of the bull, and sprinkle it on the mercy seat and before the mercy seat. So he shall make atonement for the Holy Place, because of the uncleanness of the children of Israel, and because of their transgressions, for all their sins; and so he shall do for the tabernacle of meeting which remains among them in the midst of their uncleanness. For on that day (the Day of Atonement) *the priest shall make atonement for you, to cleanse you, that you may be clean from all your sins before the Lord.*

Throughout Old Testament days, innocent animals were sacrificed, *and* their blood was sprinkled on the altar for the atonement of the sins of the Israelites to take place. Even in the New Testament era, this same principle had to be fulfilled once and forever through the blood of the Lamb of God, Yeshua, the Messiah, in order for the sins of the world to be forgiven as Hebrews 9:20-22; 24-28 tells:

*This is the blood of the covenant which God has commanded you. Then likewise he sprinkled with blood both the tabernacle and all the vessels of the ministry. And according to the law almost all things are purged with blood, and **without shedding of blood there is no remission** (Hebrews 9:20-22). For Christ has not entered the holy places made with hands, which are copies of the true, but into heaven itself, now to appear in the presence of God for us; not that He should offer Himself often, as the high priest enters the Most Holy Place every year with blood of another—He then would have had to suffer often since the foundation of the world; but now, once at the end* *of the ages, He has appeared to put away sin by the sacrifice of Himself.* ***And as it is appointed for men to die once, but after this the judgment,*** *so Christ was offered once to bear the sins of many. To those who eagerly wait for Him He will appear a second time, apart from sin, for salvation* (Hebrews 9:24-28).

Once again, God came down to His chosen kingdom and people to dwell with them. It has always been God's desire to dwell with His chosen people as their Lord, King, Savior, Deliverer, Protector, Shepherd and Friend!

THE PROPHESIES OF THE COMING OF THE MESSIAH IN THE OLD TESTAMENT AND THE FULFILLMENT IN THE NEW TESTAMENT

The Seed of the woman: The first and most important prophecy of the Messiah was recorded in Genesis 3:15 as the Seed of the woman.
Fulfillment in the New Testament: Galatians 4:4, *"But when the fullness of the time had come, God sent forth His Son, born of a woman, born under the law."*

The Son of David and Abraham: As the descendant of Abraham in Genesis 12:3, *"And in You all the families of the earth shall be blessed."* The heir to the throne of David in Isaiah 9:7, *"Of the increase of His government and peace there will be no end, upon the throne of David and over His kingdom."*

Fulfillment in the New Testament: Matthew 1:1, *"The book of the genealogy of Jesus Christ,* **the Son of David, the Son of Abraham.** *" Luke 1:32-33, "He will be great, and will be called the Son of the Highest; and* **the Lord God will give Him the throne of His father David. And He will reign over the house of Jacob forever, and of His kingdom there will be no end.***"*

Virgin birth: To be born of a virgin in Isaiah 7:14, *"Therefore the Lord Himself will give you a sign: Behold, the virgin shall conceive and bear a Son, and shall call His name Immanuel."*
Fulfillment in the New Testament: Luke 1:31-32a, *"Behold, you (Virgin Mary) will conceive in your womb and bring forth a Son, and shall call His name Jesus. He will be great, and will be called the Son of the Highest."*

The type of death: The kind of death that He would die on the Cross was vividly described in Psalm 22:16b & 18, *"They pierced My hands and My feet. They divide My garments among them, and for My clothing they cast lots."*
Fulfillment in the New Testament: As Yeshua was dying on the cross, He cried out the words in Psalm 22:1, *"My God, My God, why have You forsaken Me?"* Yeshua, the Son of the living God, was not crying out these final words because He felt separation and rejection from the Father God. Instead, Yeshua was crying out to the Israelites to prove that He was the very Messiah that the Psalmist vividly prophesied about His suffering and death in Psalm 22.

Yeshua (Jesus) declared that no one takes His life from Him but He willingly laid His life down of Himself in John 10:17-18, *"Therefore My Father loves Me, because I lay down My life that I may take it again. No one takes it from Me, but I lay it down of Myself. I have power to lay it down, and I have power to take it again. This command I have received from*

My Father." If Jesus Christ laid His life down of Himself, then there is absolutely no reason to believe that He was feeling rejection and separation from the Father on the Cross. Ultimately, it was prophesied that He will cause all the ends of the world to turn to the Lord in Psalm 22:27-31, "*All the ends of the world shall remember and turn to the Lord, and all the families of the nations shall worship before You. It will be recounted of the Lord to the next generation, they will come and declare His righteousness to a people who will be born, that He has done this.*"

Wounded for our transgressions: Isaiah 53:5, "*He was wounded for our transgressions, He was bruised for our iniquities; and by His stripes we are healed.*"
Fulfillment in the New Testament: 1 Peter 2:24, "*...who Himself bore our sins in His own body on the tree, that we, having died to sins, might live for righteousness—by whose stripes you were healed.*"

The Lord your God will raise up a Prophet: Deuteronomy 18:15, 18, "*The Lord your God will raise up for you a Prophet like me (Moses) from your midst, from your brethren. Him you shall hear.*" "*I will raise up for them a Prophet like you from among their brethren and will put My words in His mouth, and He shall speak to them all that I command Him.*"
Fulfillment in the New Testament: Luke 24:19, "*The things concerning Jesus of Nazareth, who was a Prophet mighty in deed and word before God and all the people.*"

You are My Son: Psalm 2:7-8, "*You are My Son, today I have begotten You. Ask of Me, and I will give You the nations for Your inheritance, and the ends of the earth for Your possession.*"

Fulfillment in the New Testament: Matt. 3:17, *"This is My beloved Son, in whom I am well pleased."*

THE MESSIAH AND GOD'S KINGDOM BLESSINGS

From Genesis 3:15 onward, God has promised the universal Messiah will come and eventually bring the salvation for all the families of the earth and renew His kingdom authority, power, and rule through the King of Kings and the Lord of Lords in the whole world. Messiah means *Anointed One*. Christ is the English form of the Greek *Christos*, which means also *Anointed*. *Yeshua, Jeshua,* or *Joshua* means Yahweh (Jehovah) is salvation. The English form of *Yeshua* is Jesus. We can freely use the name Jesus Christ to mean the same as Yeshua, the Messiah. The reason that the name Yeshua has been used up to this point is to prove that Yeshua in Hebrew and Jesus in English is the same name of the Messiah who is also called Christ.

God's salvation (*soteria* in Greek) will unlock the kingdom blessings throughout the Bible. When the word salvation (*yeshua* or *soteria*) is used in the Bible, it has the inclusive meanings of deliverance from sin, danger, enemy (including evil forces of darkness), and diseases so as to provide divine healing, health, prosperity, victory, safety, and welfare. The first appearance of the word salvation is recorded in Genesis 49:18, *"I have waited for your salvation, O Lord!"* It is every created human being's deep inner cry. When we find our own salvation in the Lord, then the kingdom blessings or benefits will be opened to us. The followings are some of the Scriptures that clearly describe the power and benefits of salvation:

119

When the army of Pharaoh was chasing after the Israelites who were encamped in front of the Red Sea, the Israelites cried out to Moses in Exodus 14:11-12, *"Because there were no graves in Egypt, have you taken us away to die in the wilderness? For it would have been better for us to serve the Egyptians than that we should die in the wilderness."* Once we move forward with the Lord through His divine salvation power, then we must not look or go back to our own Egyptian bondage of slavery. We must trust the power of salvation in the Lord and move forward to the Promised Land where the kingdom blessings will be flowing abundantly. Moses' response to the Israelites was written in Exodus 14:13, *"Do not be afraid.* ***Stand still, and see the salvation of the Lord,*** *which He will accomplish for you today. For the Egyptians whom you see today, you shall see again no more forever."*

What did the Israelites see as the salvation power of the Lord moving on their behalf? They witnessed God's divine protection over them and His utter destruction of the whole army of Pharaoh in action. Therefore, the salvation of God is not just a religious concept or belief of a religious order, but it is the proactive action and power of God for anyone who will put his total trust in Him for deliverance from the enemy, danger, and destruction. If we are truly in the Lord, we can see the salvation of the Lord constantly moving on behalf of us throughout the journey of life in this world.

King David understood very clearly that the Lord was his own personal salvation in Psalm 27:1, *"The Lord is my light and **my salvation (Yeshua)**; whom shall I fear? The Lord is the strength of my life; of whom shall I be afraid?"* King David, who lived under the Old Covenant, understood the true meaning of God's divine salvation power and blessings over his life. Therefore, King David was able to declare that he didn't need to fear or be afraid of anyone or anything because the Lord was not only his divine Deliverer from sin, danger, enemy, and diseases but would also provide him with prosperity, victory, safety, welfare, and health. Also, King David recognized that God's salvation had benefits for him each day, and he appropriated and enjoyed them all the days of his life. He declared in Psalm 68:19-20: *"Blessed be the Lord, **who daily loads us with benefits**, the God of our salvation! Selah. Our God is **the God of salvation**; and to God the Lord belong escapes from death."* King David understood that God of his salvation would daily load him with benefits.

The similar understanding of the kingdom benefits was revealed when Jesus Christ preached his first message in Matthew 4:17, He declared, *"Repent, for the kingdom of heaven is at hand."* As we repent of our sins, wicked ways, and lifestyles before God, the kingdom blessings or benefits will be revealed to us just as they were to David. Any ways that we are journeying in this world that are not God's ways are all wicked ways, no matter how wonderful those ways might appear to us. As we turn away from our own wicked ways and accept God's divine salvation in Jesus Christ, we will receive God's kingdom blessings, according to Psalm 103:1-5:

> *Bless the Lord, O my soul; and all that is within me bless His holy name! Bless the Lord, O my soul, and forget not **all His benefits**: who forgives all your iniquities, who heals all your diseases, who redeems your life from destruction, who crowns you with lovingkindness and tender mercies, who satisfies your mouth with good things, so that your youth is renewed like the eagle's.*

As you bless the Lord with all your soul and bless His holy name as His natural or adopted sons and daughters, He will release His divine daily benefits for His kingdom citizens to live as miracle makers and more than conquerors. In this Psalm, five benefits are mentioned:

1) **Who forgives all your iniquities**: One of the most powerful benefits of salvation is to receive God's unconditional forgiveness of all our sins, iniquities, transgressions, and trespasses that we ever committed before God and men. That's why God provided His substitutional sacrifices to pardon the sins of mankind throughout the Old Covenant. Ultimately, God sent His own Son, Jesus Christ, to pay the penalty of sin for all humanity on the Cross and provide God's salvation benefits for those who choose to believe in Him in accordance with Matthew 18:11, *"For the Son of Man has come to save that which was lost."* Once we humble ourselves and repent of all our sins before God, He will forgive all our iniquities that we have ever committed before Him. Remember that He will forgive not just some of the sins but all of our sins.

2) **Who heals all your diseases**: There were no diseases when Adam and Eve were living in the Garden of Eden. However, when they sinned before God and were cast out of the Garden, one of the curses that came upon mankind was disease. Therefore, the root cause of disease in the world can be traced back to the origination of sin. However, as we wholeheartedly turn back to God and repent of our sins, we shall receive His divine forgiveness over all our sins.

Once our sins have been forgiven, we are ready to receive God's second kingdom benefit—His divine healing over all our diseases. However, God's divine healing also depends on our obedience to His commandments and statutes, according to Exodus 15:26. Therefore, obedience is the only key that can unlock the blessings of God. Isaiah 53 is one of the most powerful prophetic chapters about the suffering Messiah. Verse five describes that Yeshua's suffering provides healing for His chosen kingdom citizens: *"But He (Yeshua) was wounded for our transgressions, He was bruised for our iniquities; the chastisement for our peace was upon Him, and by His stripes we are healed."* Because of what Yeshua, the Messiah, has done on the Cross, we not only receive God's forgiveness but also His divine healing as a free gift.

3) ***Who redeems your life from destruction***: Once we become God's children, He will not only redeem our life from destruction to endow us with abundant life in this world but also provide us with eternal life in heaven to rescue us from the eternal destruction in the lake of fire. It is God's good desire that all should come to repentance in 2 Peter 3:9, *"The Lord is not slack concerning His promise, as some count slackness, but is longsuffering toward us, not willing that any should perish but that all should come to repentance."* We can also identify God's heart for the world in John 3:16-17, *"For God so loved the world that He gave His only begotten Son, that whoever believes in Him should not perish but have everlasting life. For God did not send His Son into the world to condemn the world, but that the world through Him might be saved."*

4) ***Who crowns you with lovingkindness and tender mercies***: When you surrender your life to Jesus Christ

as your Lord and Savior, God will take away the crown of thorns upon your own head and put it on the head of Jesus on the Cross. In return, He gives you two crowns—**a crown of lovingkindness and a crown of tender mercies**. As you dwell in the house of the Lord forever, surely goodness and mercy shall follow you all the days of your life (Psalm 23:6).

5) *Who satisfies your mouth with good things so that your youth is renewed like the eagle's*: The Bible states in James 1:17, *"Every good gift and every perfect gift is from above, and comes down from the Father of lights, with whom there is no variation or shadow of turning."* God wants you to be filled with good things from above so that your youth is renewed like the eagle's each day. As we have peace with God, others, and ourselves in the world, we will be endowed with His divine good gifts that will renew our youth like the eagle's each day. We will live God's fully appointed time on the earth and no evil force of darkness will be able to shorten one second of our appointed life span.

We need to use God's five benefits each day so that we can expand the kingdom of heaven on earth as we share the message of salvation of Jesus Christ to lost souls as His obedient sons and daughters.

Chapter 7

YESHUA, THE MESSIAH (JESUS CHRIST)
THE FULFILLMENT OF THE SALVATION AND KINGDOM PLANS

⤜⥤

Yeshua came to save fallen mankind in the world as the Son of Abraham to fulfill God's covenant of Genesis 12:3 (**the Lamb of God**)—**Salvation Plan**: "And in you (Abraham) all the families of the earth shall be blessed." This Scripture was fulfilled when Jesus Christ died on the cross as the final Lamb of God to take away the sin of the world and to provide the universal salvation plan for lost humanity as the Son of Abraham. Therefore, the Bible declares in Acts 4:12, *"Nor is there salvation in any other, for there is no other name under heaven given among men by which we must be saved."*

None of the religious figures, such as Buddha, Mohammad, Hindu gods, Joseph Smith, and even Mother Mary in the world ever died and shed their own blood to redeem the fallen humanity. Only the Son of the Living God, Jesus Christ, paid the penalty of death on the cross so that whosoever calls upon the name of the Lord might be saved. Many religious people in the world dispute the fact that the Holy God had the Son through a virgin daughter of a man. Let me share with you my point of view on this matter. Let's say that you are witnessing in front of your own eyes the tragic fate of billions of ants that are dying because of wars, famine, and diseases. You want to help them, but you do not know how to help them because, as a man, you do not understand the struggles of ants. Therefore, for you to truly help the suffering ants, you need to become an ant so that you can understand their problems, suffering, and struggles as one of them. Then you might be able to provide some solution for the struggling ants. By the same token, the Holy God knows that fallen humanity is sinful and desperately wicked in all its ways.

However, God, who never committed any sin cannot truly behold Adam's sinful nature or ongoing sufferings of mankind due to the temptation of the devil. Of course, God is Omniscient, Omnipotent and Omnipresent to handle all affairs of the universe; however, He wanted to understand the struggle of mankind by becoming the perfect God and Man, Jesus Christ, the Savior of the world. Thus, the Lord allowed His Son, Jesus Christ, to be born on earth as a child through the Virgin Mary so He would experience, understand, and partake in the suffering of humanity. As a baby, Jesus had to depend completely on the care of His earthly mother.

As He grew older, He probably witnessed the suffering of His chosen people under the cruel bondage of the Roman Empire as the perfect Man. He might have also witnessed the executions of many poor and insignificant Jews who were brutally abused, tortured, and killed on the cross by the Roman soldiers. He saw the corruption of Jewish religious leaders such as High Priests, Sadducees, Pharisees, Scribes, and Rabbis of that day, and the injustice of rich against poor, orphans, widows, and the underprivileged of the society. The Bible says in Hebrews 4:15 that Jesus, as the Son of Man, was tempted in the same ways as any man: *"For we do not have a High Priest who cannot sympathize with our weaknesses, but was in all points tempted as we are, yet without sin.*" As the perfect Son of God, as well as the Son of Man, Jesus Christ lived, tasted, witnessed and partook of the torment, affliction and tribulation of fallen mankind so that He was not only able to sympathize with sinners, but also to provide the way out for fallen men through His sacrificial death on the Cross. While Jesus Christ was walking on this earth, He not only preached the kingdom of heaven but also demonstrated the power of God to set people free from the bondage of sin, sickness, curses, fear of death, and evil schemes of the devil. He healed the sick, opened the blind eyes, cleansed the lepers, cast out demons, and even raised the dead, according to Luke 4:18-19:

> *The Spirit of the Lord is upon Me, because He has anointed Me to preach the gospel to the poor; He has sent Me to heal the brokenhearted, to proclaim liberty to the captives and recovery of sight to the blind, to set at liberty those who are oppressed; to proclaim the acceptable year of the Lord.*

On the cross, Jesus Christ, the Lamb of God and Son of Abraham, paid the eternal death penalty for all humanity to provide His divine salvation plan for anyone who would call upon the name of the Lord. The Bible proclaims in Romans 3:24, "*...for all have sinned and fall short of the glory of God.*" Romans 6:23 declares, "*For the wages of sin is death, but the gift of God is eternal life in Christ Jesus our Lord.*" The purpose of the coming of Jesus Christ is summarized in both in Matthew 18:11, "*For the Son of Man has come to save that which was lost*" and in 1 John 3:8, "*He who sins is of the devil, for the devil has sinned from the beginning. **For this purpose the Son of God was manifested, that He might destroy the works of the devil.***" Before the death and resurrection of Jesus Christ, the devil had the usurped authority over the kingdoms of the world as he declared in Luke 4:5-7, *"Then the devil, taking Him up on a high mountain, showed Him all the kingdoms of the world in a moment of time. And the devil said to Him, 'All this authority I will give You, and their glory; **for this has been delivered to me, and I give it to whomever I wish.**' Therefore, if You will worship before me, all will be Yours"* When the devil claimed that he had the authority over all the kingdoms of the world, Jesus Christ didn't dispute what he said, but simply rebuked him by saying in verse 8, *"Get behind Me, Satan! For it is written, 'You shall worship the Lord your God, and Him only you shall serve.'"*

However, after His resurrection from the dead, Jesus Christ declared in Matt. 28:18-20, *"**All authority has been given to Me in heaven and on earth.** Go therefore and make disciples of all the nations, baptizing them in the name of the Father and of the Son and of the Holy Spirit, teaching them to observe all things that I have commanded you; and lo, I am with you always, even to the end of the age."*

The first man, Adam, sinned and lost to Satan the usurper, the God-ordained, divine authority to rule over the nations of the world. However, the last Adam, Jesus Christ not only paid the penalty of sin for all of fallen mankind on the cross but also took away and crucified the old man who has been infested with the first Adam's curse and sinful nature.

Therefore, whosoever calls upon the name of the Lord Jesus Christ shall be saved and those who have been baptized into Christ have been baptized into His death so that the old man has been crucified with Him. It is impossible for a sinful man to crucify his own old man on the cross so that he can be freed from sin. It was the work of Jesus Christ who took our old man to be crucified with Him on the cross so that the body of sin might be done away with, that we should no longer be slaves of sin (Romans 6:3-7). Once we accept the fact that our old man with the first Adam's sinful DNA (which released curses, sickness, unforgiveness, all forms of sinful natures, unbelief, doubt, hate, anger, pride, the devil's character and death) has been crucified with Jesus Christ, then we can also accept the truth that we have been united with Christ, the last Adam in His resurrection. Therefore, if we are in Christ, the last Adam's DNA (which releases love, joy, peace, forgiveness, blessings, abundant life, divine health, humility, provision, and eternal life) will be freely released unto us (born-again believers) by His grace.

Once we accept the fact that we are in Christ and not any longer in the first Adam, then we can freely claim the promises of Romans 8:1-2, *"There is therefore now no condemnation to **those who are in Christ Jesus**, who do not walk according to the flesh, but according to the Spirit. **For the law of the Spirit of life in Christ Jesus has made me free from the law of sin and death.**"* If we are in the first Adam, we can never walk according to the Spirit; however, if we are in Christ, there is no other choice but we have to walk according to the Spirit. It is the Christ who helps us to walk in the Spirit as He is always in the Spirit.

Jesus Christ, the perfect Son of Man reclaimed all of the authority on the earth from Satan, as He was absolutely obedient even unto death on the cross to destroy the works of the devil. It was always God's desire to dwell with His chosen people on the earth as we read in John 1:1 and 14, *"In the beginning was the Word, and the Word was with God, and the Word was God. And the Word became flesh and dwelt among us, and we beheld His glory, the glory as of the only begotten of the Father, full of grace and truth."* The Word became flesh in Jesus Christ and dwelt (*"skenoo"* in Greek which means to pitch a tent or to tabernacle) among us. It can be translated as *"the Word became flesh in Jesus Christ and pitched a tabernacle among us."* Just like the Old Testament days in the wilderness, God dwelt among His chosen people in the Tabernacle. As the Tabernacle moved, the Israelites moved. In the same sense, God dwelt or set a tabernacle in Jesus Christ in word and deed.

Wherever God moved, Jesus Christ moved and did what He saw the Father doing, according to John 5:19, *"Most assuredly, I say to you, the Son can do nothing of Himself, but what He sees the Father do; for whatever He does, the Son also does in like manner."* As the Father, Son Jesus Christ, and Holy Spirit, the triune God indwells in a Christian, his body becomes the temple of the Holy Spirit where God tabernacles in him. Therefore, wherever a believer in Christ goes, the spiritual Tabernacle of God goes with him. That also means the kingdom of God goes with him with the power of the Holy Spirit.

Jesus Christ as the perfect Son of God could not remain dead, but had to be resurrected by the power of the Holy Spirit in accordance with Romans 8:11, *"But if the Spirit of Him who raised Jesus from the dead dwells in you, He who raised Christ from the dead will also give life to your mortal bodies through His Spirit who dwells in you."* It was God, the Holy Spirit, who created Jesus in the womb of the Virgin Mary as the Son of Man (**the Son of Abraham—Salvation Plan**) and raised Jesus from the dead to inaugurate Him as the Son of God who would sit on the throne of David as the King of Kings and the Lord of Lords to expand the kingdom of heaven on earth. Therefore, He also came to re-establish God's eternal kingdom on earth as **the Son of David (the Lion of Judah)— Kingdom Plan**: Jesus Christ died on the Cross as the final Lamb of God to take away the sin of the world for the Jews and the Gentiles. However, when He arose from the grave, He didn't come back to life as the resurrected Lamb of God, but as the Lion of Judah, to sit on the throne of King David in accordance with the prophesies in Luke 1:32-33, *"He (Jesus*

*Christ) will be great, and will be called the Son of the Highest; and **the Lord God will give Him the throne of His father David.***

And He will reign over the house of Jacob forever, and of His kingdom there will be no end." Once Jesus Christ sat on the throne of David (as it was prophesied in Isaiah 9:6-7), He was ready to release His authority over the kingdoms of the world as the King of Kings, destroying the works of the devil among fallen mankind and rescuing His chosen people into the kingdom of heaven.

The very first Scripture of the New Testament (Matthew 1:1) begins with the statement, "***The Son of David, the Son of Abraham.***" The Messiah must be born to fulfill God's two redemptive plans as the Lamb and the Lion of God. As the Lamb of God, He represents the lineage of the Son of Abraham to fulfill the salvation plan of God; and as the Lion of Judah, He represents the lineage of the Son of David to reestablish God's eternal kingdom plan on earth as the King of Kings and the Lord of Lords. Jesus Christ was clearly recognized as the Lamb and Lion of God in Revelation 5:5-6:

> *"Behold, **the Lion of the tribe of Judah**, the Root of David, has prevailed to open the scroll and to loose its seven seals. And I looked, and behold, in the midst of the throne...and in the midst of the elders, stood a **Lamb** as though it had been slain."*

THE PASSOVER LAMB

Jesus Christ was God's final Passover Lamb. Just before His crucifixion, He celebrated Passover with His disciples in Luke 22:14-20. Jesus became the final Passover Lamb to take away the sins of the world once and forever. The Israelites did not need to kill any more Passover lambs to fulfill the law after the death of Jesus Christ on the Cross. Therefore, Jesus Christ was terminating the Old Testament Passover ceremony in these Scriptures and initiating the New Testament Lord's Supper to commemorate His sacrificial death on the cross as the final Passover Lamb. In Luke 22:19-20, Jesus symbolically presents His body as the sacrifice for His disciples: *"This is My body which is given for you; do this in remembrance of Me. This cup is the new covenant in My blood, which is shed for you."*

As we accept Jesus Christ as our own sacrificial Lamb for our own Passover from eternal death to eternal life and apply His blood on the doorposts of our hearts, we shall surely live, just as the Israelites were spared when they applied the blood of the Passover lamb on their physical doorposts in Egypt. In the Old Testament days, the sin of the Israelites was atoned each year by sprinkling the blood of sacrificial animals on the mercy seat of the Ark of the Covenant on the Day of Atonement in accordance with Leviticus 16:14-16:

*He shall take some of the blood of the bull and sprinkle it with his finger on **the mercy seat** on the east side; and before the mercy seat he shall sprinkle some of the blood with his finger seven times. Then he shall kill the goat of the sin offering, which is for the people, bring its blood inside the veil, do with that blood as he did with the blood of the bull, **and sprinkle it on the mercy seat** and before the mercy seat. So **he shall make atonement for the Holy Place, because of the uncleanness of the children of Israel, and because of their transgressions, for all their sins;** and so he shall do for the tabernacle of meeting which remains among them in the midst of their uncleanness.*

Therefore, the word of God in Hebrews 9:22 states, *"And according to the law almost all things are purified with blood, and without shedding of blood there is no remission."* Furthermore, during the Old Testament days, there was only one ordinance of the Passover for the Israelites, and foreigners were not allowed to take part in the ceremony according to Exodus 12:43, 47-49:

> *And the LORD said to Moses and Aaron, This is the ordinance of the Passover: **no foreigner shall eat it**. All the congregation of Israel shall keep it. And when a stranger dwells with you and wants to keep the Passover to the LORD, let all his males be circumcised, and then let him come near and keep it; and he shall be as a native of the land. For no uncircumcised person shall eat it. **One law shall be for the native-born and for the stranger who dwells among you**.*

The Old Testament order of the Passover ceremony was only applicable for the Israelites and not for the Gentiles. In order for the Gentiles to take part in the Old Testament covering of the atonement, they had to be physically circumcised and reside with the Israelites to observe every ordinance of God as the Israelites did. However, God loves not only the Jews but also the Gentiles—all the families of the world. God's divine deliverance plan revealed in Genesis 12:1-3, clearly includes the Gentiles of all the families of the earth; for it was spoken even before the Israelites were created. God created the descendants of Abraham, who would serve and worship the true one and only Creator God, so that they could be His special messenger nation to share the truth with the lost Gentiles of the earth. The true heart of God for the Gentiles was revealed throughout other Scriptures in the Old Testament:

I, the LORD, *have called You in righteousness, And will hold Your hand;* **I will keep You and give You as a covenant to the people, As a light to the Gentiles,** *To open blind eyes, To bring out prisoners from the prison, Those who sit in darkness from the prison house.* (Isaiah 42:6-7)

It is too small a thing that You should be My Servant To raise up the tribes of Jacob, And to restore the preserved ones of Israel; **I will also give You as a light to the Gentiles, That You should be My salvation to the ends of the earth.** (Isaiah 49:6)

For from the rising of the sun, even to its going down, **My name shall be great among the Gentiles;** *In every place incense shall be offered to My name, And a pure offering; For My name shall be great among the nations, says the* LORD *of hosts.* (Malachi 1:11)

God created the Israelites to shine His light to the Gentiles and His salvation to the ends of the earth. In order for God to fulfill His own prophecy in the Bible, He had to create the universal Passover Lamb so that all the families of the earth would also have the chance to be atoned of their sins. Therefore, Jesus Christ had to be born as the Son of Man, descended from the lineage of Abraham, to fulfill God's promise in Genesis 12:3, *"And in you (the Son of Abraham— Yeshua the Messiah or Jesus Christ) all the families of the earth shall be blessed."*

In his book *Eternity in their Hearts*, Don Richardson notes that people groups in the world have their distinct names for the Creator God. Their unique names became the names of God in their own Bibles instead of the Hebrew name for Almighty Yahweh. These names include: European names for the Creator—*God, Gott or Gud*; Greek and Latin names—*Deos*; The Santal people living in a region north of Calcutta, India—*Thakur Jiu* (The Genuine God); Ethiopia's Gedeo people—*Magano* (The Omnipotent Creator of all); Central African Republic's Mbaka people—*Koro* (The Creator); the Chinese—*Shang Ti* (The Lord of Heaven); and the Koreans—*Hananim* (The Great One). These names of Almighty were always in their languages and history as the Creator Yahweh had put eternity in their hearts. Therefore, the Almighty Yahweh's name has been translated into each people group's unique name for their own Almighty Creator in their own tongue in their Bibles.

However, as far as the name of the Savior Christ (Yeshua, the Messiah) is concerned in the Bibles of all of these people groups, His name has been translated into only one name under heaven as *Yeshua, Jesus or Ye Su* which originates from the name *Yeshua*. Jesus Christ declared in John 14:6, *"I am the way, the truth, and the life. No one comes to the Father except through Me."* We also read in Acts 4:12, *"Nor is there salvation in any other name under heaven given among men by which we must be saved."*

In the Old Testament days, all Israelites were commanded to take part in the Passover so that they would always remember how God brought them out of Egyptian bondage through His great signs, wonders, and miracles. The sacrificial blood of the Passover lamb that was applied on the doorpost and lintel protected the firstborn male child of the Israelites from death and destruction. The same principle has not been altered or changed in the New Testament days as well. Yahweh, the Creator God, loves the Jews as well as the Gentiles of the world. In order for Him to provide the universal salvation plan for the Gentiles, He had to provide the universal Passover Lamb who would take away the sins of the world. All of the Old Testament prophesies about the coming of the Messiah were fulfilled in Jesus Christ as the King who sat on the throne of David to usher in the kingdom of heaven on the earth.

As the final High Priest, Jesus, the Passover Lamb, took His own blood into the Holy of Holies and sprinkled that precious blood on the Mercy Seat to open the door of salvation to all the families of the earth in order to reconcile the lost sinners back to the Father God. As King, Prophet and Priest, Jesus not only preached the kingdom of heaven but also demonstrated and ushered in the kingdom power on the earth and proclaimed the coming millennium of the new heaven and earth.

IT IS FINISHED

Jesus uttered, "*It is finished!*" in John 19:30 and gave up His spirit. He came to fulfill the Old Covenant and initiated the New Covenant; thus, He said, "*It is finished!*" There was nothing more He could do for us. He paid it all for the sins of the world—for the Jews as well as for the Gentiles. Now it is our turn to accept God's divine salvation plan and live. One of the true calls of God for the Jews had been revealed in Isaiah 42:6, reiterated in Acts 13:47, "*I have set you as a light to the Gentiles, that you should be for salvation to the ends of the earth.*" Under the Old Covenant, the Gentiles were excluded from God's divine covenant blessings according to Moses' law. There was no hope for them in this life and no ability to know the true Living God of heaven and earth. The final blood sacrifice of the Lamb of God on the cross opened the door for the Gentile converts in Jesus Christ to join together with the Messianic Jews in the New Covenant. The Gentile believers of Jesus Christ were grafted into the vine of the Jews to receive the covenant blessings of Abraham as new heirs or sons of the New Covenant to enjoy God's full measure of promises according to Ephesians 2:11-18:

> *Therefore remember that you, once Gentiles in the flesh—who are called Uncircumcision by what is called the Circumcision made in the flesh by hands— that at that time you were without Christ, being aliens from the commonwealth of Israel and strangers from the covenants of promise, having no hope and without God in the world. **But now in Christ Jesus you who once were far off have been brought near by the blood of Christ.** For He Himself is our peace, who has made both one, and has broken down the middle wall of separation, having abolished in His flesh the enmity, that is, the law of command- ments contained in ordinances, so as to create in Himself one new man from the two, thus making peace, and that **He might reconcile them both to God in one body through the cross,** thereby putting to death the enmity. And He came and preached peace to you who were afar off and to those who were near. For through Him we both have access by one Spirit to the Father.*

Therefore, there is no distinction between Jew and Greek (or Gentiles), for the same Lord over all is rich to all who call upon Him as seen in Romans 10:12-13, *"For whoever calls on the name of the Lord shall be saved."* Also, the same concept of the Gentiles becoming Abraham's seed was stated in Galatians 3:26-29:

137

For you are all sons of God through faith in Christ Jesus. For as many of you as were baptized into Christ have put on Christ. There is neither Jew nor Greek, there is neither slave nor free, there is neither male nor female; for you are all one in Christ Jesus. And if you are Christ's, then you are Abraham's seed, and heirs according to the promise.

The veil of the Temple that separated the Holy of Holies from the Holy Place was torn in two. As Jesus became God's perfect sacrificial Lamb and died for the sins of Israel and the world, God tore the veil of the Holy of Holies in the Temple (Matthew 27:51). Now through the blood of Jesus Christ, who became the High Priest for the Jews as well as for the Gentiles, sons and daughters of God in the New Covenant can directly enter into the Holy of Holies, the very presence of God. So when we pray unto Yahweh, the Lord Almighty, in Jesus' name, God hears us. However, unbelieving Jews continued with animal sacrifices in accordance with the Mosaic laws in the Temple until A.D. 70. Therefore, God had to destroy His Temple to stop the Old Covenant practices of sacrificing animals while the perfect Son of God sacrificed His own blood on the Cross.

It was prophesied in Matthew 24:1-2, *"Then Jesus went out and departed from the temple, and His disciples came up to show Him the buildings of the temple. And Jesus said to them, 'Do you not see all these things? Assuredly, I say to you, not one stone shall be left here upon another, that shall not be thrown down.'"* If God would allow the Jews to practice the ways of the Old Covenant, then the death and resurrection of Jesus Christ as the perfect sacrificial Lamb of the New Covenant would have become meaningless, and the Gentiles would have remained in darkness without any hope for the remission of their sins as well as to inherit the kingdom of heaven.

GOD LOVES ALL THE FAMILIES OF THE WORLD

From the beginning of the Creation, God has always loved His created people. He wants the lost people in the world to have everlasting life through Jesus Christ, His only begotten Son according to John 3:16-21:

For God so loved the world that He gave His only begotten Son, that whoever believes in Him should not perish but have everlasting life. For God did not send His Son into the world to condemn the world, but that the world through Him might be saved. He who believes in Him is not condemned; but he who does not believe is condemned already, because he has not believed in the name of the only begotten Son of God. And this is the condemnation, that the light has come into the world, and men loved darkness rather than light, because their deeds were evil. For everyone practicing evil hates the light and does not come to the light, lest his deeds should be exposed. But he who does the truth comes to the light, that his deeds may be clearly seen, that they have been done in God.

It has always been God's desire to have intimate communion with His people. But all have sinned and fallen away from God's grace (Romans 3:23). So, He provided a way for sinners to repent and receive His forgiveness by accepting His one and only sacrificial Lamb, Jesus Christ.

Thus, John 1:12 states, *"But as many as received Him, to them He gave the right to become children of God, to those who believe in His name."* The Bible is written so that Jews and Gentiles will find Yeshua, the Messiah, or Jesus Christ, to receive the remission of their sins so that they can acquire the gift of eternal life in the kingdom of heaven. Jesus Christ is the only way for all the families of the earth, including the Jews and the Muslims, to escape from the judgment of eternal death in hell into everlasting life in heaven:

> *"These things I have written to you who believe in the name of the Son of God, that you may know that you have eternal life, and that you may continue to believe in the name of the Son of God."(1 John 5:13) "...he who hears My word and believes in Him who sent Me has everlasting life, and shall not come into judgment, but has passed from death into life."*   (John 5: 24)

THE RESURRECTION OF JESUS CHRIST

Jesus Christ said in John 11:25-26, *"I am the resurrection and the life. He who believes in Me, though he may die, he shall live. And whoever lives and believes in Me shall never die."* Do you believe this? Also, Jesus Christ prophesied His own resurrection in Matthew 27:63, *"After three days I will rise."* He arose from the dead in Matthew 28:6, *"He is not here; for He is risen, as He said."* We believe in the risen Lord. Because He lives, we can face tomorrow. He died on the cross as the Lamb of God to take away the sin of the world and to open the door of salvation to the Gentiles. He was resurrected as the Lion of Judah to bring down God's universal kingdom rule and power on earth. He rose again to initiate the New Covenant with the Jews and the Gentiles as the King of Kings and the Lord of Lords; to rule over His eternal kingdom on earth as described in the prophetic message in Revelation 11:15b, *"The kingdoms of this world have become the kingdoms of our Lord and of His Christ, and He shall reign forever and ever."*

Therefore, anyone who believes in Christ must go out and preach the message of the Lamb of God (salvation plan) to save as many lost souls as possible, and demonstrate the power of the Lion of Judah (kingdom plan), declaring that the kingdom of heaven has touched down on the earth as Matthew 10:7-8 affirms, *"And as you go, preach (salvation message), saying, 'The kingdom of heaven is at hand. Heal the sick, cleanse the lepers, raise the dead, cast out demons (demonstrating kingdom power in the name of Jesus Christ). Freely you have received, freely give."*

As we've said, all other religious figures in the world, such as Buddha, Muhammad, Hindu Gurus, Joseph Smith, and the Virgin Mary never died for the sins of the world and rose from the dead. Thus, they can neither provide salvation for mankind nor bring the kingdom of heaven on earth regardless of their religious statutes and beliefs by multitudes. They can only organize man-made religions to counterfeit what God has done for His fallen humanity. The Bible declares both in Romans 3:23, *"for all have sinned and fall short of the glory of God"* and in Romans 6:23, *"For the wages of sin is death, but the gift of God is eternal life in Christ Jesus our Lord."* Because all have sinned and the wages of sin is death, in order for fallen mankind to be delivered from eternal death in hell, the Son of Man had to die and pay for the death penalty of every lost soul in the world. As the sinless and perfect Son of Man bore upon His own body the wages of the sin of the world, He had to die to pay the penalty of death for every fallen man and woman who has ever lived and will ever live on the earth until He comes back again. Therefore, if every people, tongue, tribe and nation would accept the universal salvation plan of Jesus Christ, then they could inherit the kingdom of heaven and eternal life as a free gift. However, anyone who rejects God's divine salvation plan in Jesus Christ for his life will be lost forever, according to Revelation 20:10-15. Once Jesus or Yeshua paid the penalty of the debt for fallen mankind with His own life once and forever on the cross, He had to be resurrected as the firstfruit among the dead because the sinless Son of God cannot remain dead. Therefore, the Apostle Paul declared the order of the resurrection in 1 Corinthians 15:20-28:

> *But now Christ is risen from the dead, and has become the firstfruits of those who have fallen asleep. For since by man came death, by Man also came the resurrection of the dead. For as in Adam all die, even so in Christ all shall be made alive. But each one in his own order: Christ the firstfruits, afterward those who are Christ's at His coming. Then comes the end, when He delivers the kingdom to God the Father, when He puts an end to all rule and all authority and power. For He must reign till He has put all enemies under His feet. The last enemy that will be destroyed is death. For He has put all things under His feet. But when He says 'all things are put under Him,' it is evident that He who put all things under Him is excepted. Now when all things are made subject to Him, then the Son Himself will also be subject to Him who put all things under Him, that God may be all in all.*

The first man Adam became a living being. However, the last Adam (Jesus) became a life-giving Spirit (1 Corinthians

15:45). As Jesus Christ was resurrected to give life to those who believe in Him, those who are dead in Him will also be raised to receive an incorruptible spiritual body in the near future, as pointed out in 1 Corinthians 15:51-55:

Behold, I tell you a mystery: We shall not all sleep, but we shall all be changed—in a moment, in the twinkling of an eye, at the last trumpet. For the trumpet will sound, and the dead will be raised incorruptible, and we shall be changed. For this corruptible must put on incorruption, and this mortal must put on immortality. So when this corruptible has put on incorruption, and this mortal has put on immortality, then shall be brought to pass the saying that is written: 'Death is swallowed up in victory.' 'O Death, where is your sting? O Hades, where is your victory?'

JESUS CHRIST CONQUERED SIN, SICKNESS, CURSES, FEAR OF DEATH, AND SATAN

The greatest problem of mankind in the world is **sin**. Satan was the initiator of sin, which brought death upon all mankind. He usurped the dominion authority over the world that was given to humanity. When Adam disobeyed God's commandment and fell into the temptation of the serpent, Satan ruled the world from the fall of Adam until the death of Jesus Christ on the Cross, according to John 12:31-32, "*Now is the judgment of this world; now the ruler of this world (Satan) will be cast out. And I (Jesus Christ), if I am lifted up from the earth, will draw all peoples to Myself.*" Jesus Christ came to destroy the works and kingdom of Satan on earth in accordance with 1 John 3:8, *"He who sins is of the devil, for the devil has sinned from the beginning.* **For this purpose the Son of God was manifested, that He might destroy the works of the devil.**" After the resurrection, Jesus Christ was able to release the keys of the kingdom of heaven to the Church (each believer in Christ or the living temple of the Holy Spirit) in Matthew 16:18-19:

> *And I also say to you that you are Peter, and on this rock I will build My church, and the gates of Hades shall not prevail against it. And I will give you **the keys of the kingdom of heaven**, and whatever you bind on earth will be bound in heaven, and whatever you loose on earth will be loosed in heaven.*

Jesus Christ is the Master Key to the kingdom of heaven, and every born-again believer in Him is a duplicate key. Jesus Christ entrusts Christians to proclaim the message of the kingdom of heaven among the nations of the world because a duplicate key can open the door to the kingdom of heaven just like the Master Key. When a believer, holding the key to the kingdom of heaven, preaches the salvation and kingdom messages to unbelievers, he is able to open the kingdom of heaven to anyone who opens their heart to receive Jesus Christ as Savior and Lord.

This key to the kingdom also has the power to open any lock that Satan has bound any person with the bondage of sin and set him free in the name of Jesus Christ (Matthew 10:7-8). The only keys that Jesus Christ holds after His resurrection are the keys of Hades and of death in Revelation 1:18, *"I am He who lives, and was dead, and behold, I am alive forevermore. Amen. And I have the keys of Hades and of Death."* Therefore, Satan does not have any keys, including the keys of Hades and of death, any longer. Ultimately, Jesus Christ will open the doors to Hades and death and cast Satan, all of his demons, the beast, the false prophet, and anyone not found written in the Book of Life into the lake of fire, as Revelation 20:10-15 says:

> **And the devil, who deceived them, was cast into the lake of fire and brimstone where the beast and the false prophet are. And they will be tormented day and night forever and ever.** *Then I saw a great white throne and Him who sat on it, from whose face the earth and the heaven fled away. And there was found no place for them. And I saw the dead, small and great, standing before God, and books were opened. And another book was opened, which is* **the Book of Life**. *And the dead were judged according to their works, by the things which were written in the books. The sea gave up the dead who were in it, and Death and Hades delivered up the dead who were in them. And they were judged, each one according to his works. Then Death and Hades were cast into the lake of fire. This is the second death.* **And anyone not found written in the Book of Life was cast into the lake of fire.**

As Jesus Christ was resurrected from the grave as the Lion of Judah, He conquered sin, sickness, curses, fear of death, and Satan in order to provide His abundant life on the earth and eternal life in heaven to the children of God found in John 10:9-10, *"I am the door. If anyone enters by Me, he will be saved, and will go in and out and find pasture. The thief (Satan) does not come except to steal, and to kill, and to destroy. I have come that they may have life, and that they may have it more abundantly."*

1) ***Jesus conquered sin***: Jesus Christ came to take away the sin of the world (John 1:29). As the perfect Son of Man, He was tempted in all points as any men would be, yet without sin. *"For we do not have a High Priest who cannot sympathize with our weaknesses, but was in all points tempted as we are, yet without sin (Hebrews 4:15)." "For in that He Himself has suffered, being tempted, He is able to aid those who are tempted (Hebrews 2:18)." "No temptation has overtaken you except such as is common to man; but God is faithful, who will not allow you to be tempted beyond what you are able, but with the temptation will also make the way of escape, that you may be able to bear it"* (1 Cor. 10:13).

As the life-giving Spirit (1 Corinthians 15:45), Jesus Christ has the power to forgive the sins of all men who believe that He died on the cross for their sins and that God raised Him from the dead (Romans 10:9-10). Therefore, 1 John 1:9 declares: *"If we confess our sins, He is faithful and just to forgive us our sins and to cleanse us from all unrighteousness."* Praise be to the Lord Jesus Christ! That means Jesus Christ who conquered the power of sin as the Son of Man has authority to help anyone who will put his trust in Him to overcome sin, sinful natures, temptations, wicked evil desires, and habitual sins that came from the curses of the first Adam's DNA. However, once anyone is in Christ, the last Adam's DNA will be freely released unto him/her so that he/she will be able to walk in the Spirit to fulfill Romans 8:1-2.

2) ***Jesus conquered sickness***: There were no diseases when Adam and Eve were dwelling in the Garden of Eden. It was after they were cast out of the Garden that dreadful sickness was introduced to human beings. Therefore, sickness was introduced to all mankind through sin, the root cause of

all human problems. Once Jesus Christ destroyed the root of sin by paying the death penalty of fallen humanity on the cross, He also provided the way of deliverance from sickness through His suffering on the cross:

> *"But He was wounded for our transgressions, He was bruised for our iniquities; The chastisement for our peace was upon Him, and by His stripes we are healed* (Isaiah 53:5)." *"...who Himself bore our sins in His own body on the tree, that we, having died to sins, might live for righteousness--by whose stripes you were healed* (1 Peter 2:24)."

According to 1 Peter 2:24, *"**having died to sins**"* is the prerequisite for living in righteousness and receiving God's divine healing. You may ask what *"having died to sins"* means. It is an ongoing process of sanctification after one becomes a born-again believer in Christ. Through the power of the Holy Spirit, a believer must accept the fact that his/her old man was crucified with Jesus Christ when he/she was baptized into Christ Jesus so that he/she is not any more under the curses of the first Adam but under the blessings of the last Adam, Jesus Christ.

Therefore, a believer in Christ must declare the promises in Romans 6:3-7 each day or whenever he/she falls into the temptation to be back into the first Adam so that he/she can fulfill the process of having died to sins as the Apostle Paul described in Romans 6:3-7, *"Or do you not know that **as many of us as were baptized into Christ Jesus were baptized into His death**? Therefore **we were buried with Him through baptism into death**, that just as Christ was raised from the dead by the glory of the Father, even so **we also should walk in newness of life**. For if we have been united together in the likeness of His death, certainly **we also shall be in the**

*likeness of His resurrection, knowing this, that **our old man
was crucified with Him, that the body of sin might be done
away with,** that we should no longer be slaves of sin. **For he
who has died has been freed from sin.**"* As we fully
appropriate the prerequisite for receiving God's divine healing
according to the above Scriptures, then the result will be—**by
Jesus Christ's stripes we are healed.**

Jesus Christ began His public ministry in Matthew 4:23-
24 by demonstrating three aspects of His divine anointing: 1)
teaching, 2) preaching, and 3) healing all kinds of sickness:

> *And Jesus went about all Galilee, **teaching** in their
> synagogues, **preaching** the gospel of the kingdom, and
> **healing all kinds of sickness and all kinds of disease**
> among the people. Then His fame went throughout all
> Syria; and they brought to Him all sick people who
> were afflicted with various diseases and torments, and
> those who were demon-possessed, epileptics, and
> paralytics; and He healed them.*

After Jesus Christ called His twelve disciples in Luke
6:12-13, He gave them power and authority over all demons
and to cure diseases in Luke 9:1-2, *"Then He called His
twelve disciples together and **gave them power and authority**
over all demons, and **to cure diseases.** He sent them to preach
the kingdom of God and **to heal the sick.**"* It is amazing that
Jesus Christ had only just chosen these twelve men to be His
disciples in Luke 6, yet He gave them His divine power and
authority over all demons and diseases in Luke 9.
Chronologically speaking, between Luke 6 and 9 was a very
short time.

This event happened before Jesus Christ's death on the
cross, His resurrection and witnessing the day of Pentecost
when the power of the Holy Spirit came down upon the one

hundred and twenty believers. Jesus chose these twelve apostles not because they were perfect or qualified men; Peter denied Jesus Christ three times. Thomas doubted the resurrected Lord until he touched His wounds. James and John asked Jesus Christ to grant one of them to sit at His right hand and the other at His left hand when He would come in His glory. Judas betrayed Him for thirty pieces of silver. Nevertheless, He chose them by His grace and gave them His authority and power over demons and disease to glorify the Lord. When Jesus appointed seventy others, who were not apostles but common followers in Luke 10:1, to declare the kingdom of God, He also commanded them to heal the sick in Luke 10:9. He gave them **the authority over all the power of the enemy** in Luke 10:17-20:

> *And **heal the sick** there, and say to them, 'The kingdom of God has come near to you.'" "Then the seventy returned with joy, saying, 'Lord, even the demons are subject to us in Your name.' And He said to them, 'I saw Satan fall like lightning from heaven. Behold, I give you **the authority to trample on serpents and scorpions, and over all the power of the enemy**, and nothing shall by any means hurt you. Nevertheless do not rejoice in this, that the spirits are subject to you, but rather rejoice because your names are written in heaven.'*

It is remarkable that Jesus Christ used the novice apostles as well as seventy common followers to have His authority over all the power of the enemy, and to cure diseases before His death, resurrection and the coming of the Holy Spirit. Then, **how much more Jesus Christ wants to use New Covenant followers, those who know the power of the Cross, the resurrection of Christ, and the baptism of the**

Holy Spirit, to demonstrate His salvation plan and kingdom plan; to save lost souls, heal the sick and cast demons out of those who are under the bondage of the power of the devil. Even under the Old Covenant, God expressed His desire to bring healing upon His chosen people as they would obey His commandments, statutes, laws, and judgments, according to Exodus 15:26 and Psalm 103:3.

Therefore, if we diligently obey the voice of the Lord our God and do what is right in His sight, then He will provide us with His divine health as we go through the journey of this short life. However, if we become sick, we can boldly ask the Lord to forgive all our sins and to heal us according to His perfect will. Then, we shall receive His divine healing in faith. We can also pray for anyone who is sick to be healed, according to His commandment in Matthew 10:7-8 and James 5:14-15, *"Is anyone among you sick? Let him call for the elders of the church, and let them pray over him, anointing him with oil in the name of the Lord. And the prayer of faith will save the sick, and the Lord will raise him up. And if he has committed sins, he will be forgiven."*

3) *Jesus Conquered Curses*: The first curse recorded in the Bible is against the serpent by God in Genesis 3:14-15, and is followed by the curses upon the woman and the man in verses 16-19. Also, in Genesis 2:16-17, the Lord warns Adam of the curse of death. As the first man, Adam sinned before God. The curse of death became a reality, as in Genesis 3:19, *"In the sweat of your face you shall eat bread till you return to the ground, for out of it you were taken; for dust you are, and to dust you shall return."* Yahweh, the Almighty God, established His sovereign blessings and curses based on how anyone treated the descendants of Abraham in Genesis 12:3, *"I will **bless those who bless you, and I will curse him who curses you**; and in you all the families of the earth shall be*

blessed." Anyone and any nation that blesses the nation of Israel and the Jews, God will render His divine blessings on them.

God also declared the long list of curses in Deuteronomy 28:15-68 (54 verses of curses) over the Israelites, His chosen people, if they would not obey His voice. However, God also provided blessings for those who would obey His voice in Deuteronomy 28:1-14. Therefore, God is the Author of blessings and curses over mankind in the Bible. As we have learned, Satan does not have his own inherent power to bring curses upon God's created mankind. God Himself had already cursed Satan, the old serpent. The curse upon the devil cannot be revoked or altered, and it is the eternal curse that will be culminated in the lake of fire in the future. The devil knows the curse that has been pronounced against him and on fallen mankind by the Lord.

The devil's tactics against fallen humanity have always been to tempt or entice people to sin against the established order, statutes, judgments, commandments, and laws of the Lord with a disobedient heart so that God's wrath can fall upon them; eventually their sin will lead them to the eternal hell fire. This is why the devil will do anything to cause one of God's chosen children to fall away from Him through manipulating him/her with constant lies and distortions. In order to deliver fallen mankind from curses and release the blessing of Abraham, Jesus Christ had to become a curse for people in accordance with Galatians 3:13-14, *"Christ has redeemed us from the curse of the law, having become a curse for us (for it is written, 'Cursed is everyone who hangs on a tree'), that the blessing of Abraham might come upon the Gentiles in Christ Jesus, that we might receive the promise of the Spirit through faith."*

Therefore, if anyone is in Christ Jesus, His substitutional death on the cross removes God's curses that were upon him.

This is done through the blood of His only begotten Son, the final Passover Lamb. Through Jesus Christ (the Son of Abraham), God's blessings that were promised to Abraham's descendants will also flow into the Gentile believers because they became adopted children of God. He also eliminated any generational curses as well as any other curses that anyone might have spoken against the children of God. As you become a child of God, you will enjoy God's divine blessings and abundant life on earth and the eternal life in the kingdom of heaven.

4) ***Jesus Christ conquered the fear of death***: Jesus Christ declared in John 11:25-26, "***I am the resurrection and the life. He who believes in Me, though he may die, he shall live. And whoever lives and believes in Me shall never die. Do you believe this?***" Jesus Christ is Resurrection and He is Life. Even before the miracle of Christ's own resurrection from the grave, He demonstrated His resurrection power by raising the dead daughter of Jairus back to life in Mark 5:21-24, 35-42; the dead son of a widow of Nain back to life in Luke 7:11-15; and the dead Lazarus back to life in John 11:38-44.

Jesus Christ is the perfect Son of Man and the Son of God. He is the Creator of life and all other things according to Colossians 1:16-17, "*For by Him all things were created that are in heaven and that are on earth, visible and invisible, whether thrones or dominions or principalities or powers. All things were created through Him and for Him. And He is before all things, and in Him all things consist.*" Jesus Christ declared that He has life in Himself in John 5:26, "*For as the Father has life in Himself, so He has granted the Son to have life in Himself.*" Therefore, no power in heaven and earth and under the earth can take away His divine life. This is why Jesus Christ declared that He laid down His own life for the sheep in John 10:15. When Jesus Christ took upon His own body the sins of all humanity, the Son of Man decided to lay His life down to pay for the penalty of sin with His own death. However, the sinless Son of God could not remain in the grave, so God the Holy Spirit raised Him from the dead, just as Romans 8:11 records: *"But if the Spirit of Him who raised Jesus from the dead dwells in you, He who raised Christ from the dead will also give life to your mortal bodies through His Spirit who dwells in you."*

Even though Jesus Christ had to die for the sins of the world, the grave and death were not able to hold Him down because He was the sinless Son of Man and God. The death, resurrection, and ascension of Christ secured forever the final authority for Jesus (Matthew 28:18). That authority has been extended to all believers in the Great Commission so that we may continue His work of destroying the works of the devil (1 John 3:8). Through the resurrection power of Jesus Christ, we can also live in freedom from the law of sin and death as in Romans 8:2, *"For the law of the Spirit of life in Christ Jesus has made me free from the law of sin and death."* Also, Romans 6:9 states, *"Christ, having been raised from the dead, dies no more. Death no longer has dominion over Him."*

Thus, Jesus Christ said in John 16:33, *"In the world you will have tribulation; but be of good cheer, I have overcome the world."* Jesus Christ is the Firstfruit of resurrection among the saints who have fallen asleep. Through His death and resurrection, He has also secured the resurrection and eternal life for the rest of the saints as 1 Corinthians 15:20-23 states:

But now Christ is risen from the dead, and has become the firstfruits of those who have fallen asleep. For since by man came death, by Man also came the resurrection of the dead. For as in Adam all die, even so in Christ all shall be made alive. But each one in his own order: Christ the firstfruits, afterward those who are Christ's at His coming.

The Bible prophesies that the final victory for the saints who have been dead, as well as who are alive in Christ, will be their transformation into incorruptible bodies, according to 1 Corinthians 15:50-57:

Now this I say, brethren, that flesh and blood cannot inherit the kingdom of God; nor does corruption inherit incorruption. Behold, I tell you a mystery: We shall not all sleep, but we shall all be changed--in a moment, in the twinkling of an eye, at the last trumpet. For the trumpet will sound, and the dead will be raised incorruptible, and we shall be changed. For this corruptible must put on incorruption, and this mortal must put on immortality. So when this corruptible has put on incorruption, and this mortal has put on immortality, then shall be brought to pass the saying that is written: 'Death is swallowed up in victory.' 'O Death, where is your sting? O Hades, where is your victory?' The sting of death is sin, and the strength of sin is the law. But thanks be to God, who gives us the victory through our Lord Jesus Christ.

A similar account is recorded in 1 Thessalonians 4:13-18:

But I do not want you to be ignorant, brethren, concerning those who have fallen asleep, lest you sorrow as others who have no hope. For if we believe that Jesus died and rose again, even so God will bring with Him those who sleep in Jesus. For this we say to *you by the word of the Lord, that we who are alive and remain until the coming of the Lord will by no means precede those who are asleep. For the Lord Himself will descend from heaven with a shout, with the voice of an archangel, and with the trumpet of God. And **the dead in Christ will rise first. Then we who are alive and remain shall be caught up together with them in the clouds to meet the Lord in the air.** And thus we shall always be with the Lord. Therefore comfort one another with these words.*

Jesus Christ fully experienced and overcame the pain, agony, separation, shame, suffering, and fear of death on the cross as the perfect Man. Now the resurrected Lord Jesus Christ declares in Matthew 28:18, *"All authority has been given to Me in heaven and on earth."* Therefore, He has divine power to help all the sons and daughters of God to overcome any fear associated with death on the earth. He has not given us a spirit of fear, but of power, love, and a sound mind (2 Timothy 1:7). Now we can boldly declare, *"Though we walk through the valley of the shadow of death, we will fear no evil; for the Lord Jesus Christ is with us."* Therefore, saints must not fear death on this earth. Death is the door to the eternal kingdom of heaven. As our physical body dies, our spirit will immediately be with the Lord Jesus Christ in His Paradise in heaven.

5) *Jesus Christ conquered Satan*: Ultimately, Jesus Christ, as the Son of Man, conquered Satan. This means He now has all power over Satan's wicked and evil schemes, tactics, plans, temptations, intentions, and ways against God's elect or chosen people. We can truly declare in faith and with the absolute confidence in our heart the promise in Romans 8:31, *"If God is for us, who can be against us?"* No power of

Satan can overcome the children of God because of God's promises in Romans 8:32-39:

He who did not spare His own Son, but delivered Him up for us all, how shall He not with Him also freely give us all things? Who shall bring a charge against God's elect? It is God who justifies. Who is he who condemns? It is Christ who died, and further-more is also risen, who is even at the right hand of God, who also makes intercession for us. Who shall separate us from the love of Christ? Shall tribulation, or distress, or persecution, or famine, or nakedness, or peril, or sword? As it is written: 'For Your sake we are killed all day long; we are accounted as sheep for the slaughter.' **Yet in all these things we are more than conquerors through Him who loved us. For I am persuaded that neither death nor life, nor angels nor principalities nor powers, nor things present nor things to come, nor height nor depth, nor any other created thing, shall be able to separate us from the love of God which is in Christ Jesus our Lord.**

The Lord also disarmed principalities and powers, making a public spectacle of them and triumphed over them (Colossians 2:15). When we are living under the certain bondage of sin, we are allowing principalities, powers, and demonic evil forces of darkness to bind us to do the will of the deceiver, Satan. However, once we have been set free by committing our life to Jesus Christ, He will deliver us from the power of Satan to God by disarming all associated demonic hierarchical bondage over us. Therefore, a former cocaine addict, prostitute, liar, adulterer, alcoholic, sexual pervert, fornicator, homosexual, and even a murderer can become God's saint through the blood of Jesus Christ. Satan's final fate unfolds in Revelation 20:10, *"And the devil, who deceived them, was cast into the lake of fire and brimstone where the beast and the false prophet are. And they will be tormented day and night forever and ever."*

If you have surrendered your life to Jesus Christ, then He dwells within you with all authority over Satan on this earth (Matthew 28:18). Jesus Christ is the Miracle-Maker, and with Him you can do all things. The Miracle-Maker who dwells in you wants you to become a miracle-maker for His glory to destroy the works of the devil. We must not make the Mighty Miracle-Maker in us to be a powerless and religious god in our lives but allow Him to manifest out of us so that He can set the lost, broken, and bound people free from the power of Satan.

Therefore, Jesus Christ fulfilled God's divine salvation plan as the final Passover Lamb to take away the sin of the world and to draw the Jews as well as the Gentiles back to Yahweh, the one and only Creator of the heavens and earth. Once Jesus Christ paid the death penalty for all humanity on the cross, He arose from the grave to establish the kingdom of God on the earth as the King of Kings and the Lord of Lords to expand His kingdom throughout the world. He entrusts His kingdom work on earth to the children of God through the power of the Holy Spirit, according to Matthew 10:7-8; 28:18-20 and Acts 1:8. The simple qualification to become sons and daughters of God is written in John 1:12-13, *"But as many as received Him (Yeshua or Jesus Christ) to them He gave the right to become children of God, to those who believe in His name: who were born, not of blood, nor of the will of the flesh, nor of the will of man, but of God."*

Chapter 8

JESUS CHRIST: THE MEDIATOR BETWEEN GOD AND MAN

Having accomplished all the requirements of God to become the Mediator between God and man, Jesus Christ became the Great High Priest to reconcile all the lost sinners in the world back to the Creator God. He sprinkled His own blood on the Mercy Seat of God to provide God's divine atonement for the sin of the world so that whosoever calls upon the name of the Lord Jesus Christ can be saved. This is why when Jesus Christ died on the cross, the veil of the Temple, separating the Holy Place from the Holy of Holies, was torn in two from top to bottom (Matthew 27:51).

This opened the door of salvation not only for the Jews, but also for the Gentiles of the world. Jesus Christ terminated the Old Testament order of the High Priest system that was only available to the Jews. When the acting high priests died due to their limited life span on the earth, a new high priest had to be inaugurated to replace the dead one. Therefore, Jesus Christ initiated and became the New Testament order of the High Priest for all humanity, every people, tongue, tribe and nation, as the eternal and perpetual One who will never die again as in Hebrews 4:15-16, *"For we do not have a High Priest who cannot sympathize with our weaknesses, but was in all points tempted as we are, yet without sin. Let us therefore come boldly to the throne of grace, that we may obtain mercy and find grace to help in time of need."*

THE GREAT HIGH PRIEST

Jesus Christ became the Great High Priest according to the order of Melchizedek. In order for us to understand the order of the new priesthood, we need to study Hebrews 7:

*For this Melchizedek, king of Salem, **priest of the Most High God**, who met Abraham returning from the slaughter of the kings and blessed him, to whom also Abraham gave a tenth part of all, first being translated 'king of righteousness,' and then also king of Salem, meaning 'king of peace,' **without father, without mother, without genealogy, having neither beginning of days nor end of life, but made like the Son of God**, remains a priest continually. Now consider how great this man was, to whom even the patriarch Abraham gave a tenth of the spoils. And indeed those who are of the sons of Levi, who receive the priesthood, have a commandment to receive tithes from the people according to the law, that is, from their brethren, though they have come from the loins of Abraham; but he whose genealogy is not derived from them received tithes from Abraham and blessed him who had the promises. Now beyond all contradiction the lesser is blessed by the better. Here mortal men receive tithes, but there he receives them,* *of whom it is witnessed that he lives. Even Levi, who receives tithes, paid tithes through Abraham, so to speak, for he was still in the loins of his father when Melchizedek met him. Therefore, if perfection were through the Levitical priesthood (for under it the people received the law), what further need was there that **another priest should rise according to the order of Melchizedek**, and not be called according to the order of Aaron? For the priesthood being changed, of necessity there is also a change of the law. For He of whom these things are spoken belongs to another tribe, from which no man has officiated at the altar. For it is evident that our Lord arose from Judah, of which tribe Moses spoke nothing concerning priesthood. And it is yet far more evident if, in the likeness of Melchizedek, **there arises another priest** who has come, not according to the law of a fleshly commandment, but **according to the power of an endless life**. For He testifies: 'You are a priest forever according to the order of Melchizedek.' For on the one hand there is an annulling of the former commandment because of its weakness and unprofitableness, for the law made nothing prefect; on the other hand, there is the bringing in of a better hope, through which we draw near to God. And inasmuch as He was not made priest without an oath (for they have become priests without an oath, but He with an oath by Him who said to Him: "The Lord has sworn and will not relent, **'You are a priest forever according to the order of Melchizedek'**"), by so much more Jesus has become a surety of a better covenant. Also there were many priests, because they were prevented by death from continuing. But He, because He continues forever, has an unchangeable priesthood. Therefore*

He is also able to save to the uttermost those who come to God through Him, since He always lives to make intercession for them. *For such a High Priest was fitting for us, separate from sinners, and has become higher than the heavens; who does not need daily, as those high priests, to offer up sacrifices, first for His own sins and then for the people's, for this He did once for all when He offered up Himself. For the law appoints as high priests men who have weakness, but the word of the oath, which came after the law, appoints the Son who has been perfected forever.*

Hebrews 7:14-17 describes, *"Our Lord (Jesus Christ) arose from (the tribe of) Judah, of which tribe Moses spoke nothing concerning priesthood. And it is yet far more evident if, in the likeness of Melchizedek, there arises another priest who has come, not according to the law of a fleshly commandment, but according to the power of an endless life. For He testifies; 'You are a priest forever according to the order of Melchizedek.'"* Therefore, Jesus Christ has become a surety of a better covenant and the only perfect Mediator between God and men (Hebrews 7:23-27) to provide the atonement for sins not only for the Jews but also for the Gentiles. Now, whosoever calls upon the name of the Lord Jesus Christ can receive the remission of sins through the High Priest who stands forever before God with His own atoning blood to take away the sin of the world.

THE WAGES OF SIN IS DEATH

Why then do we need the Savior, the One and only Lord Jesus Christ (Yeshua), and not any other gods? Jesus Christ is the only perfect Son of God and Son of Man who died on the cross to pay the death penalty of sin for all humanity to rescue us from eternal condemnation in hell fire. The word of God declares in John 8:24, *"Therefore I said to you that you will die in your sins; for if you do not believe that I am He, you will die in your sins."* Also, Romans 3:23 states, *"for all have sinned and fall short of the glory of God."* Ever since Adam and Eve committed sin before God, all their descendants inherited their sinful nature (DNA) from birth. Therefore, Romans 6:23 declares: *"For the wages of sin is death, but the gift of God is eternal life in Christ Jesus our Lord."* This means that the wages for anyone who dies in their own sin will not only bring physical death on the earth but also eternal death in hell forever and ever. Ultimately, sinners will be judged by God and be cast into the lake of fire as recorded in Revelation 20:11-15.

However, it is not God's will that any should perish with his own sins but that all should come to repentance (2 Peter 3:9) so that they can inherit the kingdom of heaven. God did not create this sin-infested, cursed, troubled, and diseased world originally. He initially created a perfect paradise (the Garden of Eden) where there was no death, sickness, sorrow, war, curses, or separation from Him. Sin caused mankind to inherit this cursed world. Nevertheless, God has never forgotten His original plan for all humanity to dwell in His paradise for eternity. Therefore, God provided the perfect substitutional Lamb who would pay the penalty of sin for all humanity in order to bring those who would believe in Him into eternal paradise—the kingdom of heaven.

Now only two choices are available for fallen humanity according to the decree of the Creator God: 1) fallen men have to pay for their sins eternally in hell or 2) accepts the Lamb of God—Jesus Christ's death on the cross—for the remission of their sins and receive God's divine kingdom and salvation plans. Then, we can live for His glory as God's chosen children on the earth and receive His eternal life back in the Paradise. However, billions of people have been deceived by the lies of the devil. Some believe that they will be reincarnated after death. Others believe that life on earth is the only tangible one, and they will simply go back to the dust and simply not exist anymore after death. Yet others believe that they can directly go to a paradise by killing innocent lives as jihad in the name of their god.

However, the Bible, the very authority of the word of the Creator God, declares that the dead will be judged according to their works. The Bible says in Hebrews 9:27, "*And as it is appointed for men to die once, but after this the judgment.*" If anyone dies in his own sins, he shall surely pay the penalty of sin eternally in hell. Will you believe the lies of the devil or the word of the Living God? Choose life this day and live according to Deuteronomy 30:15-20:

*See, **I have set before you today life and good, death and evil**, in that I command you today to love the Lord your God, to walk in His ways, and to keep His commandments, His statutes, and His judgments, that you may live and multiply; and the Lord your God will bless you in the land which you go to possess. But if your heart turns away so that you do not hear, and are drawn away, and worship other gods and serve them, I announce to you today that you shall surely perish; you shall not prolong your days in the land which you cross over the Jordan to go in and possess. I call heaven and earth as witnesses today against you, that **I have set before you life and death, blessing and cursing; therefore choose life**, that both you and your descendants may live; that you may love the Lord your God, that you may obey His voice, and that you may*

163

*cling to Him, for **He is your life and the length of your days**; and that you may dwell in the land which the Lord swore to your fathers, to Abraham, Isaac, and Jacob, to give them.*

ETERNAL LIFE—THE GIFT OF GOD

The Lord is not willing that any should perish but that all should come to repentance and be saved (2 Peter 3:9). Whoever calls on the name of the Lord shall be saved (Acts 2:21) and the gift of God is eternal life in Christ Jesus our Lord (Romans 6:23). There are three cries for souls described in Scripture; from heaven, from the world and from hell.

The first cry is from heaven: Yahweh, the Creator God, calls from heaven in Isaiah 6:8, *"'Whom shall I send, and who will go for Us?' Then I (Isaiah) said, 'Here am I! Send me.'"* Also the Bible declares in Isaiah 52:7, *"How beautiful upon the mountains are the feet of him who brings good news, who proclaims peace, who brings glad tidings of good things, who proclaims salvation, who says to Zion, 'Your God reigns!'"* Yahweh desires to proclaim His good news to the ends of the world so that every people, tribe, tongue, and nation can hear the message of salvation and turn away from their wicked ways to find abundant life on earth and eternal life in the kingdom of heaven.

The Joshua Project estimates that there are now over 3,200 people groups larger than 10,000 in size in which there is no witnessing church movement capable of reaching its own people within these groups. Therefore, we must do everything we can to introduce God's salvation plan to these unreached people groups in the world so that the kingdom of heaven and all of its associated blessings can be extended into them. The will of Yeshua for the world is very clear in Matthew 24:14, *"And this gospel of the kingdom will be preached in all the world as a witness to all the nations, and then the end will come."* According to this Scripture, the end of the ages and the Second Coming of Christ (1 Thessalonians 4:13-18) will only occur when the gospel will be preached among all the unreached people groups in the world. That is why the Apostle Paul declared in Romans 15:20, *"And so I have made it my aim to preach the gospel, not where Christ was named, lest I should build on another man's foundation."* Thus, every disciple of Yeshua must obey the command in Isaiah 6:8 and go and evangelize as many unreached people groups as we can. If you are not called to go, then support mission organizations that are fulfilling the Great Commission to bring God's salvation and kingdom plans to unreached people groups in the world.

The second cry is from this world (Acts 16:25-30): While the Apostle Paul and Silas were praying and singing hymns to God in prison, a great earthquake opened the doors of the prison and loosed everyone's chains. When the keeper of the prison thought that the prisoners had fled, he was going to kill himself. However, when Paul called and let him know that they did not escape out of prison, the keeper brought them out and asked in Acts 16:30, *"Sirs, what must I do to be saved?"* Paul and Silas said in verse 31, *"Believe on the Lord Jesus Christ, and you will be saved, you and your household."* Multitudes of people in the world are seeking honestly to find the answer to the same question. *"What must I do to be saved?"*

As I have traveled to over ninety countries to share the gospel of Jesus Christ, I have often asked the following question to a Hindu, Buddhist, Muslim, secular humanist, and animist: *"If you were to die today, do you know where you are going?"* The most common answers were, *"I don't know."* To satisfy their quests for salvation (i.e. to have an eternal life in paradise), they are trying to worship or buy their way to heaven by serving or worshiping religious orders, objects, idols, philosophies, traditions, religious ideas of men, animals as gods, stars, sun, moon, mountains, and trees. The religions of the world cause their followers to rely on man-made ways, religious rituals, and traditions to appease God's wrath over their sins. Eventually, they hope to reach up to God in heaven or paradise. However, the Creator God's salvation and kingdom plans have been initiated by Him in order to reach down from the kingdom of heaven to the lost souls in the world so that they can find eternal life by accepting the death, burial and resurrection of His divine sacrificial Lamb who came to take away the sins of the fallen mankind.

The third cry is from the pit of hell (Luke 16:19-31):

*There was a certain rich man who was clothed in purple and fine linen and fared sumptuously every day. But there was a certain beggar named Lazarus, full of sores, who was laid at his gate, desiring to be fed with the crumbs which fell from the rich man's table. Moreover the dogs came and licked his sores. So it was **that the beggar died, and was carried by the angels to Abraham's bosom.** The rich man also **died and was buried.** And **being in torments in Hades,** he lifted up his eyes and saw Abraham afar off, and Lazarus in his bosom. Then he cried and said, 'Father Abraham, have mercy on me, and send Lazarus that he may dip the tip of his finger in water and cool my tongue; for I am tormented in this flame.' But Abraham said, 'Son, remember that in your lifetime* *you received your good things, and likewise Lazarus evil things; but now he is comforted and you are tormented. And besides all this, between us and you there is a great gulf fixed, so that those who want to pass from here to you cannot, nor can those from there pass to us.' Then he said, '**I beg you therefore, father, that you would send him to my father's house, for I have five brothers, that he may testify to them, lest they also come to this place of torment.**' Abraham said to him, 'They have Moses and the prophets; let them hear them.' And he said, 'No, father Abraham; but if one goes to them from the dead, they will repent.' But he said to him, 'If they do not hear Moses and the prophets, neither will they be persuaded though one rise from the dead.'*

In these Scriptures, the rich man who went to Hades to be tormented forever, cried out from Hades to Father Abraham and asked Him to send Lazarus back to his (the rich man's) house. The rich man, who knew the lifestyle of his five other brothers, was very much concerned that the same fate would fall on them in Hades for eternity after their deaths. He began to cry out to Abraham in Hades in verse 27: "*I beg you therefore, father, that you would send him (Lazarus) to my father's house, for I have five brothers, that he may testify to them, lest they also come to this place of torment.*"

I believe that billions of people in hell are crying out to Jesus Christ to send someone to testify to their loved ones who are living in sin on this earth every day. They may be dead on earth but live eternally in the torment of hell fire forever and ever, and their hearts have been broken over their loved ones when they have finally realized the truth of the Bible. All those who are in hell truly understand the truth of the gospel of Jesus Christ as the only Savior and Lord, but it is too late for them to save themselves. Now then, what must one do to be saved? The Bible says in Romans 6:23, *"For the wages of sin is death, but the gift of God is eternal life in Christ Jesus our Lord."* If eternal life in Christ Jesus is a free gift from God, then we must simply receive Him in faith as our Lord and Savior. We cannot work to achieve eternal life or pay for it with good deeds, according to Ephesians 2:8-9, *"For by grace you have been saved through faith, and that not of yourselves; it is the gift of God, not of works, lest anyone should boast."*

Many self-proclaimed good people, who declare that they have never killed, hurt, abused, misused and robbed anyone, committed sexual sins, or taken advantage of the poor, weak, and helpless orphans and widows say that they will go to heaven after their death because they believe that they have been good.

However, the word of God says that if you broke one law, you have broken all laws as found in James 2:10, *"For whoever shall keep the whole law, and yet stumble in one point, he is guilty of all."* Also, Ecclesiastes 7:20 states, *"For there is not a just man on earth who does good and does not sin."* This means there are no good people on earth who can go to heaven based on their own goodness, no matter how good they may perceive themselves to be.

We must accept the fact that Christ Jesus paid for our sins on the Cross and died. On the third day, He rose from the dead and He ascended to the right hand of the Father God. We must follow the most practical guide in the New Testament for accepting the Lord Jesus Christ as our Lord and Savior as described in Romans 10:9-10, *"If you confess with your mouth the Lord Jesus and believe in your heart that God has raised Him from the dead, you will be saved. For with the heart one believes to righteousness, and with the mouth confession is made to salvation."* We must repent of our sins and confess that Jesus Christ is our Lord and Savior in accordance with 1 John 1:9, *"If we confess our sins, He is faithful and just to forgive us our sins and to cleanse us from all unrighteousness."* We also must believe in Jesus Christ alone for our salvation because He is the only One who died on the cross as God's final Passover Lamb to take away the sin of the world. Therefore the Apostle Paul declares in Acts 4:12, *"Nor is there salvation in any other, for there is no other name under heaven given among men by which we must be saved."*

This is your moment to accept Jesus Christ, Yeshua Ha-Mashiach, as your personal Lord and Savior for your eternal salvation! Surrender your life to Yeshua Ha-Mashiach if you are a Jew, to Isa al-Masih (Jesus Christ in Arabic) if you are a Muslim, or to Jesus Christ, if you are the rest of the Gentiles and follow Him for the rest of your life. Then, His abundant life (a life that is full of His divine spiritual peace, joy, and love) will be poured into you while you are living in this short life on earth. Eternal life in heaven will be granted to you after your death on earth. Please pray the following prayer and believe in Jesus Christ, the Lamb of God. Receive Him in your heart for the forgiveness of your sins. Then you will be saved and have eternal life now.

Dear Lord! I am a sinner. I repent of my sins and turn away from my wicked ways. Please forgive all my sins and cleanse me with the precious blood of Jesus Christ. Come into my heart and be my Lord and Savior. I surrender my whole life to You. Write my name in the Lamb's Book of Life. I now receive eternal life in faith. Please fill me with the Holy Spirit and guide my life according to Your perfect will and purpose from this moment on. Thank you for forgiving all my sins and accepting me as your child. Jesus Christ, You are my Lord and Savior. From this day on, anoint me to live for Your glory and fulfill Your call and divine purpose for my life. Help me to obey the Great Commission in Matthew 28:18-20 and Acts 1:8. Thank you Lord! I pray in the name of Jesus Christ or Yeshua Ha-Mashiach. Amen.

Chapter 9

NEXT STEPS TO FOLLOW

⎯⎯⎯⎯⎯

Once anyone is born again and becomes a citizen of the kingdom of heaven, there are important steps to follow in order to enlighten one's new relationship with the Lord. A newborn believer must read the Bible daily and bring every concerned matter to the Lord in prayer. Especially, a new Christian needs to learn how to hear the still small voice of the Holy Spirit to know the perfect will of God for his/her life. Let the Holy Spirit lead him/her to find a suitable local church where he/she can grow in the Lord and have fellowship with other believers in Christ.

Why does a new Christian need to read the word of God daily? The Lord provides the best answer in Psalm 1:1-3, *"Blessed is the man who walks not in the counsel of the ungodly, nor stands in the path of sinners, nor sits in the seat of the scornful; but his delight is in the law of the Lord, **and in His law he meditates day and night. He shall be like a tree planted by the rivers of water, that brings forth its fruit in its season, whose leaf also shall not wither; and whatever he does shall prosper.**"* Anyone who reads and meditates on the word of God day and night will reap the blessing of prosperity in whatever he does. Another similar promise is written in Joshua 1:8: *"This Book of the Law shall not depart from your* *mouth, but **you shall meditate in it day and night**, that you may observe to do according to all that is written in it. For **then you will make your way prosperous, and then you will have good success**.*" As you meditate in the Book of the Law day and night and do according to all that is written in it (**obey the word of God and apply His principles in your life daily**), then you will make your way prosperous and have good success in what you do. These are great promises to obey and follow if we want to be prosperous in whatever we do.

Why does a new Christian need to hear the still small voice of the Holy Spirit through prayer? The perfect answer is found in Mathew 7:7-8 and John 16:13-15:

*Ask, and it will be given to you; **seek**, and you will find; **knock**, and it will be opened to you. For everyone who asks **receives**, and he who seeks **finds**, and to him who knocks it will be **opened**.*
(Matthew 7:7-8)

*However, when He, the Spirit of truth, has come, **He will guide** you into all truth; for He will not speak on His own authority, but whatever He hears **He will speak**; and **He will tell** you things to come. He will glorify Me, for He will take of what is Mine and declare it to you. All things that the Father has are Mine. Therefore I said that **He will take of Mine and declare it to you**.*
(John 16:13-15)

Jesus Christ is clearly recommending for believers to ask, seek, and knock in prayer, and then they will receive and find their answers from God. The door, which will carry the answers to prayers, will be opened wide for them. Jesus Christ declares that when we pray in the Spirit, the Holy Spirit will guide believers into all truth, speak what He hears from the Lord, tell of things to come, and declare what is of Him. It is not going to be Jesus Christ who will guide, speak, tell, and declare to us, but the Holy Spirit will. If the Holy Spirit is going to guide believers into all truth, then they must talk with Him. If the Holy Spirit is going to speak to believers, then they must listen to Him. If the Holy Spirit is going to tell believers about the things to come in the future, then they need to hear Him. This means believers in Christ must have constant communion with the Holy Spirit about all matters dealing with their lives on the earth.

Why does a new believer need to have fellowship with other believers in a local church? The best answer can be found in Acts 2:42-47 which mentions **eight blessings** of taking part in a local church:

> *And they continued steadfastly in the apostles' **doctrine and fellowship**, in the **breaking of bread**, and in **prayers**. Then fear came upon every soul, and **many wonders and signs were done** through the apostles. Now all who believed were together, and had **all things in common**, and sold their possessions and goods, and **divided them among all, as anyone had need**. So continuing daily with one accord in the temple, and breaking bread from house to house, they ate their food with gladness and simplicity of heart, **praising God** and having favor with all the people. And **the Lord added to the church daily those who were being saved.***

The eight blessings for believers becoming a part of the first local church in Jerusalem were specifically described:

1) They received regular instruction as they continued steadfastly in the apostles' doctrine.
2) They enjoyed ongoing fellowship with other believers.
3) They took part in church ordinances—"breaking of bread."
4) They were covered by corporate prayers.
5) They experienced supernatural signs and wonders by the ministries of the apostles.
6) Their needs were met by sharing and receiving of goods.
7) They were able to express their love for God in corporate praise and worship.
8) They witnessed the divine growth of the church daily.

WATER BAPTISM

After we become a believer in Christ and a child of the Living God, we need to sever our sinful relationship with the world and declare our new allegiance to God as His living witness. We must accept the fact that Jesus Christ crucified our old man with Himself on the cross in order to set us free from the bondage of being in the first Adam's curse and DNA (Romans 6:3-6): such as shame, guilt, addiction to sinful desires, bitterness, anger, condemnation, judgment, curses, sicknesses, fear, doubt, unbelief, self-condemnation, unloving spirit, sexual immorality, covetousness, lust of the eyes, lust of the flesh and pride of life, etc.

At the same token, we also must accept the truth and declare in faith the word of God in Romans 6:5-6 has been done in our lives if we are in Christ, the last Adam: *"For if we have been **united together in the likeness of His death,** certainly we also shall be **in the likeness of His resurrection,*** *knowing this, that **our old man was crucified with Him**, that the body of sin might be done away with, that we should no longer be slaves of sin.*" Therefore, we are a new creation in Christ according to 2 Corinthians 5:17, "*Therefore, if anyone is in Christ, he is a new creation; old things have passed away; behold, all things have become new.*" If we are in Christ, the last Adam, we are also entitled to receive all the blessings that the last Adam's DNA releases into our lives: such as abundant life (John 10:10b), blessings from a life-giving spirit (1 Corinthians 15:45), His resurrection power and life (John 11:25), love, joy, peace, divine health, and seven provisions of Jesus Christ in Revelation 5:12, "*Worthy is the Lamb who was slain to receive **power** and **riches** and **wisdom**, and **strength** and **honor** and **glory** and **blessing!**"*

As we go through the ceremony of water baptism, we are symbolically accepting the truth that our old sinful man has been crucified with Christ. When we come out of the water, we are declaring to the world that we will live with the risen Lord for the rest of our lives for His glory and honor according to His good and perfect will. This is the meaning of water baptism according to Romans 6:1-14. As we believe that we have been crucified with Jesus Christ on the cross, we are acknowledging the fact that He took all our sins upon Himself so that we can be set free from the curse and power of sin. Once we fully understand the benefits of Jesus' death on the cross, then we are ready to enjoy His divine blessings of the power of resurrection in our lives. After receiving Jesus Christ as our Lord and Savior, we should be baptized in water as soon as possible. Eight important provisions will follow after going through water baptism:

1) We are **baptized into Jesus' Death** in Romans 6:3, "*Do you know that as many of us as were baptized into Christ Jesus were baptized into His death?*"

2) We **walk in newness of life** in Romans 6:4, *"Therefore we were buried with Him through baptism into death, that just as Christ was raised from the dead by the glory of the Father, even so we also should walk in newness of life."*

3) **Our old man was crucified with Jesus** in Romans 6:5-6, *"For if we have been united together in the likeness of His death, certainly we also shall be in the likeness of His resurrection, knowing this, that our old man was crucified with Him, that the body of sin might be done away with, that we should no longer be slaves of sin."*

4) We are **freed from sin** in Romans 6:7, *"For he who has died has been freed from sin."*

5) **We shall live with Jesus** in Romans 6:8-9, *"Now if we died with Christ, we believe that we shall also live with Him, knowing that Christ, having been raised from the dead, dies no more. Death no longer has dominion over Him."*

6) We are **alive to God** in Romans 6:11, *"Likewise you also, reckon yourselves to be dead indeed to sin, but alive to God in Christ Jesus our Lord."*

7) **We present our members as instruments of righteousness to God** in Romans 6:12-13, *"And do not present your members as instruments of unrighteousness to sin, but present yourselves to God as being alive from the dead, and your members as instruments of righteousness to God."*

If we do all the above, **the final provision** will be available to us:

8) **Sin shall not have dominion over us** in Romans 6:14, *"For sin shall not have dominion over you, for you are not under law but under grace."*

THE LORD'S SUPPER

The Lord Jesus Christ commanded the believers to observe the Lord's Supper in remembrance of His sacrificial death for the sin of the world. The Lord's Supper replaced the Old Testament ceremony of the Passover in Luke 22:15-16, *"With fervent desire I have desired to eat this Passover with you before I suffer; for I say to you, I will no longer eat of it until it is fulfilled in the kingdom of God."*

As He became the final Passover Lamb who died on the Cross once and for all for the sin of the world, the Israelites did not need to sacrifice any more Passover lambs to fulfill the Old Testament covenant. In fact, the event in Luke 22:7-20 was the termination of the Old Testament ceremony of Passover and the initiation of the New Testament ceremony of the Lord's Supper. The Lord's Supper replaced the Passover as Jesus Christ became the fulfillment of the New Covenant as the final Passover Lamb. Thus, Jesus Christ is called as the Lamb of God in John 1:29, *"Behold! The Lamb of God who takes away the sin of the world!"*

Transferring the ordinance of the Passover from the Old Covenant ritual to the New Covenant Lord's Supper in Christ Jesus is clearly described in Hebrews 9:1-15:

Then indeed, even the first covenant had ordinances of divine service and the earthly sanctuary. For a tabernacle was prepared: the first part, in which was the lampstand, the table, and the showbread, which is called the sanctuary; and behind the second veil, the part of the tabernacle which is called the Holiest of All, which had the golden censer and the ark of the covenant overlaid on all sides with gold, in which were the golden pot that had the manna, Aaron's rod that budded, and the tablets of the covenant; and above it were the cherubim of glory overshadowing the mercy seat. Of these things we cannot now speak in detail. Now when these things had been thus prepared, the priests always went into the first part of the tabernacle, performing the services. But into the second part the high priest went alone once a year, not without blood, which he offered for himself and for the people's sins committed in ignorance; the Holy Spirit indicating this, that the way into the Holiest of All was not yet made manifest while the first tabernacle was still standing. It was symbolic for the present time in which both gifts and sacrifices are offered which cannot make him who performed the service perfect in regard to the conscience—concerned only with foods and drinks, various washings, and fleshly ordinances imposed until the time of reformation. But Christ came as High Priest of the good things to come, with the greater and more perfect tabernacle not made with hands, that is, not of this creation. **Not with the blood of goats and calves, but with His own blood He entered the Most Holy Place once for all, having obtained eternal redemption.** *For if the blood of bulls and goats and the ashes of a heifer, sprinkling the unclean, sanctifies for the purifying of the flesh,* **how much more shall the blood of Christ, who through the eternal Spirit offered Himself without spot to God, cleanse your conscience from dead works to serve the living God?** *And for this reason* **He is the Mediator of the new covenant,** *by means of death, for the redemption of the transgressions under the first covenant, that those who are called may receive the promise of the eternal inheritance.*

Furthermore, Hebrews 9:22b states, "*And according to the law almost all things are purged with blood, and without shedding of blood there is no remission.*" Through the shedding of the precious blood of the Lamb of God, He provided anyone who calls upon the name of the Lord to be saved and receive the remission of his sins which entitles him to take the Lord's Supper in accordance with Matt. 26:26-28, "*Jesus took bread, blessed it and broke it, and gave it to the disciples and said, 'Take, eat; this is My body.' Then He took the cup, and gave thanks, and gave it to them, saying, 'Drink from it, all of you. For this is My blood of the new covenant, which is shed for many for the remission of sins.'*"

As we take part in the Lord's Supper, we must adhere to the following two instructions to honor what He has done for us:

1) ***Proclaim the Lord's death*** according to 1 Corinthians 11:26, "*For as often as you eat this bread and drink this cup, you proclaim the Lord's death till He comes*"

2) ***Examine yourself before partaking the Lord's Supper*** according to 1 Corinthians 11:29-30, "*For he who eats and drinks in an unworthy manner eats and drinks judgment to himself, not discerning the Lord's body. For this reason many are weak and sick among you, and many sleep.*"

The word of God declares that the life of the flesh is in the blood (Leviticus 17:11). The natural blood that flows through our veins provides life to the living beings. By the same token, in order for anyone to have abundant life on earth and eternal life in heaven, symbolically speaking, we must have the transfusion of the blood of the Lamb of God by repenting from our sins before God, accepting the sacrificial death of the Lord Jesus Christ on the cross for sins. No other blood in this world can save us from our sins, except the Lamb of God who shed His own blood on the cross to provide God's divine salvation plan for the fallen sinners.

OUTPOURING OF THE HOLY SPIRIT

The finished work of redemption through Jesus Christ on the cross was the prerequisite for the outpouring of the Holy Spirit. Thus, the coming of the Holy Spirit follows the completion of God's gracious redeeming work in the life, death and resurrection of Jesus Christ, the Son of God. The coming of the Holy Spirit is the direct fulfillment of the promise of God. On the day of Pentecost, Peter defended the disciples in Jerusalem who had just received the gift of the Holy Spirit and said: *"This is what was spoken by the prophet Joel: 'And in the last days it shall be, God declares, that I will pour out my Spirit upon all flesh '"* (Acts 2:16-17). We clearly need to understand the kingdom purpose for the coming of God, the Holy Spirit, upon believers of Jesus Christ. Unfortunately, the body of Christ has been divided over the minor issues of the baptism with the Holy Spirit.

1) Some believe that when anyone receives Jesus Christ as his Lord and Savior, the baptism of the Holy Spirit takes place at the same time. Since the Holy Spirit comes into believers at the time of salvation experience, they believe that a newborn believer doesn't need to seek the baptism of the Holy Spirit at a later date. However, if they truly believe that they were baptized with the Holy Spirit when they accepted the Lord, then why they do not practice or manifest the gifts of the Holy Spirit in the lives that are described in

1 Corinthians 12:4-11:

There are diversities of gifts, but the same Spirit. There are differences of ministries, but the same Lord. And there are diversities of activities, but it is the same God who works all in all. **But the manifestation of the Spirit is given to each one for the profit of all:** *for to one is given the* **word of wisdom** *through the Spirit, to another the* **word of knowledge** *through the same Spirit, to another* **faith** *by the same Spirit, to another* **gifts of healings** *by the same Spirit, to another the* **working of miracles,** *to another* **prophecy,** *to another* **discerning of spirits,** *to another* **different kinds of tongues,** *to another the* **interpret-tation of tongues.**

If they proclaim that they are full of the Holy Spirit since their conversion to Christ, then they should freely speak in tongues, exercise the gifts of healings, perform miracles, prophesy, or discern the work of different spirits on a regular basis. The reality is that those who believe this hardly ever obey or practice 1 Corinthians 12:8-11. Also, anyone who professed to speak in tongues was branded as doing the work of the devil, according to the teachings of Christian leaders among many fundamental denominational churches. If we follow this camp's advice, then we are agreeing that the Scriptures dealing with the gifts of the Holy Spirit, such as the word of wisdom and knowledge, faith, gifts of healings, working of miracles, prophecy, discerning of spirits, different kinds of tongues, and the interpretation of tongues, are erroneous and not applicable to the modern times.

Hebrews 13:8 speaks very clearly that Jesus Christ is the same yesterday, today, and forever. If Jesus never changes in His manifestation, power, and glory, why has the work of the

Holy Spirit, who is the Spirit of Jesus Christ and the Father God, been dramatically reduced in scope and power among certain members of the body of Christ? If they claim to have been baptized in the Holy Spirit when they were born again, then they must exercise the gifts of the Holy Spirit inside and outside of the Church to expand the kingdom of God, according to Acts 1:8 and demonstrate the kingdom power as specified by Matthew 10:7-8.

2) ***Others believe that one's salvation experience and the baptism of the Holy Spirit are two distinct and separate occurrences.*** However, the same group believes that the baptism of the Holy Spirit must be followed by the manifestation of speaking in an unknown tongue. In this camp, even though one may have a powerful experience of the Holy Spirit, if he is not speaking in tongue, he is considered not baptized in the Holy Spirit. Therefore, the emphasis of the baptism with the Holy Spirit rests solely on the tangible manifestation of speaking in tongues and not on the transformation of the whole person by the power of the Holy Spirit. Some have said, *"We must follow the exact example of the Bible. In the Scriptures, after they were baptized in the Holy Spirit, they spoke in tongues (meaning unknown language)."*

This statement is not based on the absolute truth. First of all, Jesus Christ didn't speak in tongues after He was baptized in the Holy Spirit. Instead, the Father God spoke in Matthew 3:17, *"This is My beloved Son, in whom I am well pleased."* Secondly, the one hundred and twenty disciples who were mightily baptized in the Holy Spirit on the day of Pentecost spoke the message of the Holy Spirit to those visitors from sixteen different people groups in Jerusalem in the visitors' own languages according to Acts 2:11, *"We hear them speaking in our own tongues the wonderful works of God."*

Thirdly, Samaritan Christians who received the baptism of the Holy Spirit, after they believed in Jesus Christ and received water baptism, didn't speak in tongues right away (Acts 8:14-17). Only Gentiles in Caesarea and the disciples in Ephesus spoke in tongues after they received the Holy Spirit in Acts 10:23-48 and 19:1-6. When Saul was baptized in the Holy Spirit, he didn't speak in tongues right away but his scales fell from his eyes and he received his sight at once and he arose and was baptized (Acts 9:10-19).

Therefore, the notion that we must speak in tongues as the evidence of our baptism in the Holy Spirit is not biblically correct. The apostle Paul asked a rhetorical question in 1 Corinthians 12:30-31. *"Do all have gifts of healings? Do all speak with tongues? Do all interpret? But earnestly desire the best gifts."* According to this Scripture, not all believers who have been baptized with the Holy Spirit will speak with tongues. However, the Apostle Paul also emphasizes in 1 Corinthians 14:39, *"Therefore, brethren, desire earnestly to prophesy, and do not forbid to speak with tongues."* It is very clear that speaking with tongues is one of the gifts of the Holy Spirit. If so, we must not forbid anyone to speak with tongues who is led by the power of the Holy Spirit either.

3) *The biblically correct version describes that the salvation in Jesus Christ and sealing of the Holy Spirit take place when one surrenders one's life to Jesus as one's Lord and Savior.* However, the baptism with the Holy Spirit normally takes place after the salvation experience. The Triune God, Father, Son, and Holy Spirit exists as One in Trinity. Therefore, when anyone surrenders one's heart to Jesus Christ and becomes a born-again believer, the Triune God enters and dwells in him/her to seal him/her as the son or daughter of God, according to John 14:16-17, 20, 23:

183

And I will pray the Father, and He will give you another Helper, that He may abide with you forever, even the Spirit of truth, whom the world cannot receive, because it neither sees Him nor knows Him; but you know Him, for He dwells with you and will be in you (John 14:16-17). ***At that day you will know that I am in My Father, and you in Me, and I in you*** (John 14:20). *If anyone loves Me, he will keep My word; and My Father will love him, and We will come to him and make Our home with him* (John 14:23).

However, the Holy Spirit, who comes into a believer with Jesus Christ and the Father as the part of the Triune God at the time of conversion, does not constitute as the baptism with the Holy Spirit to empower one to become His witness in the dark world. According to consistent examples of the Bible, the baptism with the Holy Spirit took place after the conversion of a believer, except the simultaneous case of Jesus' baptism with the Holy Spirit.

How Jesus received the baptism with the Holy Spirit: The Bible describes the conception of Jesus in Matthew 1:18, *"Now the birth of Jesus Christ was as follows: After His mother Mary was betrothed to Joseph, before they came together, she was found with **child of the Holy Spirit**."* Jesus, the Son of Joseph and Mary, was conceived by the power of the Holy Spirit. This means the Holy Spirit was in Jesus from the moment of conception in Mary's womb. Even though the Holy Spirit was in Jesus, the Son of Man, He didn't do any work of the kingdom of God or perform any miracles when He remained as the Son of Joseph and Mary. When Jesus was baptized by John the Baptist, He not only experienced water baptism but also empowerment by the Holy Spirit (or baptism with the Holy Spirit without speaking unknown tongues). At the same time, a voice came from heaven, saying, *"This is My beloved Son, in whom I am well pleased* (Matthew 3:17)." All four gospels identically describe the event of Jesus' baptism in the Holy Spirit in the following manner: Matthew 3:16, *"He saw the Spirit of God descending like a dove and* **alighting upon Him***."* Mark 1:10, *"He saw the heavens parting and the Spirit* **descending upon Him** *like a dove."* Luke 3:22, *"And the Holy Spirit descended in bodily form like a dove* **upon Him***."* John 1:32, *"I saw the Spirit descending from heaven like a dove, and He* **remained upon Him***."*

It is obvious that the Holy Spirit did not come into Jesus Christ but rested upon Him. Shortly after the Holy Spirit came down upon Jesus (even though the Holy Spirit was already in Him), He was led by the Spirit into the wilderness to be tempted by the devil for forty days. After Jesus overcame all the temptations of the devil, then He returned in **the power of the Spirit** to Galilee. From that point on, Jesus was not anymore recognized as the Son of Joseph and Mary but as the Anointed One, Christ, or Messiah. **Only after Jesus Himself was baptized in the Holy Spirit, He began to preach and teach about the kingdom of God, to heal multitudes of sick, and deliver numerous people who had been bound by unclean spirits and demons—even legions of them.** Jesus, Son of Man or Son of Joseph and Mary, became Jesus Christ, the Son of God, after the baptism of the Holy Spirit to fulfill the Old Testament prophecy in Isaiah 61:1-2 that was reiterated in Luke 4:18-19:

The Spirit of the Lord is **upon Me***, because He has* **anointed Me** *to preach the gospel to the poor. He has sent Me to heal the brokenhearted, to preach deliverance to the captives and recovery of sight to the blind, to set at liberty those who are oppressed, to preach the acceptable year of the Lord.*

Therefore, we can conclude that the Holy Spirit in Jesus Christ didn't anoint Him to preach, minister, or perform any miracles as He faithfully remained as the Son of Joseph and Mary to take care of the household business as a carpenter. It was the baptism with the Holy Spirit that was described as *"The Spirit of the Lord is upon Me"* that released the full power and anointing for Him to preach, teach, and minister deliverance to the lost and dying humanity.

How the first disciples received the Holy Spirit: We can identify in John 20:22 that Jesus Christ appeared to His disciples after the resurrection. He breathed on them and said to them, *"Receive the Holy Spirit."* At that moment, the Holy Spirit entered into them and sealed them as God's chosen children. We can say that they were truly born again from that point on. Therefore, the Spirit of Christ must be indwelled in a believer to be considered as a son or daughter of God, according to Romans 8:9 & 14, *"But you are not in the flesh but in the Spirit, if indeed the Spirit of God dwells in you. Now if anyone does not have the Spirit of Christ, he is not His. For as many as are led by the Spirit of God, these are sons of God."*

The Holy Spirit in you seals you as God's special inheritance according to Ephesians 1:13-14:

*In Him you also trusted, after you heard the word of truth, the gospel of your salvation; in whom also, having believed, **you were sealed with the Holy Spirit of promise**, who is the guarantee of our inheritance until the redemption of the purchased possession, to the praise of His glory.*

Before Jesus Christ ascended to heaven, He gave the Great Commission to the same disciples in Matthew 28:18-20 and Acts 1:8:

All authority has been given to Me in heaven and on earth. Go therefore and make disciples of all the nations, baptizing them in the name of the Father and of the Son and of the Holy Spirit, teaching them to observe all things that I have commanded you; and lo, I am with you always, even to the end of the age.
(Matthew 28:18-20)
*But you shall receive power when the Holy Spirit has come **upon** you; and you shall be witnesses to Me in Jerusalem, and in all Judea and Samaria, and to the end of the earth.* (Acts 1:8)

However, Jesus Christ commanded them not to depart from Jerusalem but to wait for the promise of the Father in Acts 1:4-5, *"You have heard from Me; for John truly baptized with water, but you shall be **baptized with the Holy Spirit** not many days from now."* By this point, they were truly born again and received the Holy Spirit in them (John 20:22). However, they needed the baptism with the Holy Spirit who would empower them to carry out the Great Commission to the ends of the world. Even though these disciples walked with Jesus Christ for three years and witnessed His preaching, healings, deliverances, death on the Cross, and resurrection, they were still not fully qualified to go into the world to minister until they received the baptism with the Holy Spirit.

Pentecost (Shavuot in Hebrew)—The Feast of Weeks: On the day of Pentecost, the disciples and believers were all filled with the Holy Spirit as the event was described in Acts 2:2-4, *"And suddenly there came a sound from heaven, as of a* *rushing mighty wind, and it filled the whole house where they were sitting. Then there appeared to them divided tongues, as of fire, and one sat upon each of them. And they were all filled with the Holy Spirit and began to speak with other tongues, as the Spirit gave them utterance.*" As Jesus Christ declared in Acts 1:8, the one hundred and twenty believers who were in the upper room (Acts 1:13) were mightily baptized with the Holy Spirit and became ready to carry out the Great Commission from Jerusalem to the ends of the earth.

Jesus Christ is the Firstfruit, according to 1 Corinthians 15:20, *"But now Christ is risen from the dead, and has become the firstfruits of those who have fallen asleep."* The Messiah of the world, Jesus Christ, rose again on the third day (literally, the third day of Passover week) on the day of the Firstfruits. Kevin Howard and Marvin Rosenthal's book *The Feasts of the Lord* describes, *"The resurrection of Jesus Christ had far greater implications. Paul explained, 'For as in Adam all die, even so in Christ all shall be made alive' (1 Corinthians 15:22). The resurrection of Jesus is the guarantee and the beginning (firstfruits) of the final harvest, or resurrection, of all mankind. The Messiah fulfilled the prophetic meaning of this holy day by rising from the dead to become the firstfruits of the resurrection, and He did it on the very day of Firstfruits."*

In a way, the resurrected Lord Jesus Christ dedicated His firstfruits unto the Father God on the day of Pentecost, and, in turn, the Creator God, Yahweh responded by sending the promise of the Holy Spirit to baptize or consume the firstfruits of the one hundred and twenty disciples with His holy fire. Therefore, it was evident that these followers who already believed in Jesus Christ were baptized with the Holy Spirit at a later date—on the day of Pentecost—as Christ's firstfruits to the Lord. Again, only after they were baptized with the power of the Holy Spirit were they able to carry out the Great

Commission from Jerusalem to the ends of the earth with signs, wonders, and miracles following.

The disciples in Samaria (Acts 8:5-17): Philip, one of original seven deacons, went down to the city of Samaria and preached Christ to the Samaritans. The Bible describes his ministry in Samaria in verses 6-8 and 12, "*And the multitudes with one accord heeded the things spoken by Philip, hearing and seeing the miracles which he did. For unclean spirits, crying with a loud voice, came out of many who were possessed; and many who were paralyzed and lame were healed. And there was great joy in that city. But when they believed Philip as he preached the things concerning the kingdom of God and the name of Jesus Christ, both men and women were baptized.*"

It is very clear that Philip, who was not one of the first apostles but a deacon, was able to perform many signs, wonders, and miracles in the name of Jesus Christ in Samaria. Therefore, the notion of God's miraculous healings ending after the death of the original apostles is not biblically correct. If a young deacon was able to heal many sick people without the presence of the apostles, anyone who believes in Christ can do the same. Furthermore, it is obvious that Samaritan believers didn't receive the baptism with the Holy Spirit when they accepted the salvation message of Christ through Philip's preaching. They were baptized with the Holy Spirit when Peter and John laid hands on them in Acts 8:14-17:

*Now when the apostles who were at Jerusalem heard that Samaria had received the word of God, they sent Peter and John to them, who, when they had come down, prayed for them that they might receive the Holy Spirit. For as yet He had fallen **upon** none of them. They had only been baptized in the name of the*

Lord Jesus. Then they laid hands on them, and they received the Holy Spirit.

It is also clear that Samaritan believers did not speak in tongues after they had been baptized with the Holy Spirit. Therefore, we cannot make a statement that if anyone is baptized with the Holy Spirit, he must speak in tongues as the evidence.

Saul's conversion and baptism with the Holy Spirit (Acts 9:1-19): Saul was a persecutor of believers in Christ. While he was going to Damascus to find more believers to bring them bound to Jerusalem, he had a divine encounter with the Lord Jesus Christ. A light shone around him from heaven and blinded him. The Lord told him to go into the city where he would be instructed what he had to do (verses 1-6). In the meantime, the Lord directed Ananias to go and find Saul and pray for him so that Saul could receive his sight back and be filled with the Holy Spirit as written in verses 17-18, *"Brother Saul, the Lord Jesus, who appeared to you on the road as you came, has sent me that you may receive your sight and be filled with the Holy Spirit. Immediately there fell from his eyes something like scales, and he received his sight at once; and he arose and was baptized."*

In Saul's case, he received the baptism with the Holy Spirit followed by the water baptism. The Bible did not relate that Saul spoke with tongues immediately after the baptism with the Holy Spirit. However, Saul whose name became Paul, definitely spoke with tongues later as found in 1 Corinthians 14:18, *"I thank my God I speak with tongues more than you all."*

The Gentiles in Caesarea (Acts 10:23-48): Cornelius a centurion of the Italian Regiment was a devout man and one who feared God with all his household. He gave alms generously to the people and prayed to God always (Acts 10:1-2). Even though he was a God-fearing man of prayer, he was not a born-again believer of Jesus Christ. God sent an angel and instructed Cornelius to send men to the apostle Peter in Joppa who would tell him what he had to do (Acts 10: 3-6). Eventually Peter came and preached the gospel to Cornelius' household in Acts 10: 44-48:

> *While Peter was still speaking these words, the Holy Spirit fell upon all those who heard the word. And those of the circumcision who believed were astonished, as many as came with Peter, because the gift of the Holy Spirit had been poured out on the Gentiles also. For they heard them speak with tongues and magnify God. Then Peter answered, 'Can anyone forbid water, that these should not be baptized who have received the Holy Spirit just as we have?' And he commanded them to be baptized in the name of the Lord.*

In this case, followers were first baptized with the Holy Spirit as they believed the word of Peter, and they spoke with tongues. Then they went through the water baptism in Christ's name.

The disciples in Ephesus (Acts 19:1-6): When the apostle Paul found some disciples in Ephesus, the first thing that he asked them about was the issue of the baptism with the Holy Spirit:

> *And it happened, while Apollos was at Corinth, that Paul, having passed through the upper regions, came to Ephesus. And finding some disciples he said to*

*them, 'Did you receive the Holy Spirit when you believed?' So they said to him, 'We have not so much as heard whether there is a Holy Spirit.' And he said to them, 'Into what then were you baptized?' So they said, 'Into John's baptism.' Then Paul said, 'John indeed baptized with a baptism of repentance, saying to the people that they should believe on Him who would come after him, that is, on Christ Jesus.' When they heard this, they were baptized in the name of the Lord Jesus. And when Paul had laid hands on them, **the Holy Spirit came upon them, and they spoke with tongues and prophesied.***

In this case, the disciples in Ephesus were only baptized into John's baptism—a baptism of repentance. Once they understood that they needed to believe on the Lord Jesus Christ, they were baptized once again in the name of Christ. After their second water baptism in Christ, they were baptized with the Holy Spirit, spoke with tongues, and prophesied. Here we can see very clearly that Paul was ministering to the Gentile believers in Ephesus to receive the baptism of the Holy Spirit after believing in Jesus Christ.

Chapter 10

THE WORK OF THE HOLY SPIRIT

⟨⟩

The main purpose of the coming of the Holy Spirit is clearly described in John 16:8, *"And when He (The Holy Spirit) has come, He will convict the world of sin, and of righteousness, and of judgment."* God, the Holy Spirit, is coming to you so that He can empower you to become a witness of Jesus Christ in your own Jerusalem and to the ends of the world (Acts 1:8). His anointing and power in your life through the baptism of the Holy Spirit will cause you to shine the fruit as well as the gifts of the Spirit to convict the world of sin, of righteousness, and of judgment.

We are living between the era after the coming of the Holy Spirit on the day of Pentecost and the Second Coming of Jesus Christ. God, the Holy Spirit, is here to empower His chosen people to fulfill God's Great Commission in Matthew 28:18-20, Mark 16:15-18, Luke 24:46-48, and Acts 1:8 until the prophecy of Matthew 24:14 is fulfilled: *"And this gospel of the kingdom will be preached in all the world as a witness to all the nations (Greek [ethne]: all the ethnic people groups), and then the end will come."* So let's go back to the beginning of the Bible. Originally, the Father God created the Garden of Eden where mankind would have the perfect harmony with the Lord and dwell in His presence eternally. God's divine purpose for Adam and Eve was for them to have dominion over every living thing on the earth (Genesis 1:28). However, the fall of mankind caused them to be cast out of the paradise into this cursed world where sin, sickness, curses, wars, poverty, disasters, death, demons and the bondage of darkness reign. Throughout the Old Testament days, the Father God provided His divine laws, statutes and commandments for His chosen people to live by so that the world would know that the One and Only true living God indwelled with His people. The law of God was given to His chosen people so that they would not sin against Him. Because the wages of sin is death, and without the shedding of blood there is no remission of sin (Romans 6:23 and Hebrews 9:22). Therefore, God sent His own Son to be the propitiation for our sins. The Bible declares in 1 John 3:8, "*For this purpose the Son of God was manifested, that He might destroy the works of the devil.*"

Jesus Christ, the last Adam came to set the captives free from the bondages of sin, sickness, curses, the fear of death, and Satan. Jesus came to die on the cross as the Lamb of God to take away the sin of the world, but He was raised from the dead as the Lion of Judah to establish the kingdom of heaven on the earth as the King of Kings and the Lord of Lords. Jesus Christ declared in Matthew 28:18, "*All authority has been given to Me in heaven and on earth.*" This means Satan has no authority in heaven and on earth. The last Adam took away the usurped authority of Satan as the prince of this world once and forever. Jesus Christ came to bring the kingdom of heaven down to the earth so that His chosen people would live according to the word of God to expand His kingdom in the world. In order for the Father God and His Son, Jesus Christ to utilize the fallen mankind as His chosen saints to expand the kingdom of God on earth, the Holy Spirit has to come and empower them to fulfill the Great Commission. When we become born-again Christians, we are sealed with the Holy Spirit who will reside in us as the guarantee of our inheritance so that we can be seated with Christ in heaven. In a way, when the Holy Spirit comes into a believer, He will elevate his position from an orphan to a child of God who will inherit the kingdom of heaven. However, when a believer is baptized with the Holy Spirit, He brings the kingdom authority of Jesus Christ and the power of God from heaven to the earth to fulfill the mission of Jesus Christ that He had accomplished on the Cross—**to destroy the works of the devil**.

As we become believers in Christ, the authority of Jesus will be available to us to do the work of the kingdom of God. When we are baptized with the Holy Spirit, the power of God becomes available to us to destroy the works of the devil in the name of Jesus Christ. Therefore, every born-again believer stands between Jesus Christ (the Authority) and the Holy Spirit (the Power). Without a believer exercising God's ordained authority of Jesus Christ to preach the kingdom of God, to heal the sick, or to cast out demons in faith, the power of the Holy Spirit will not be released. A believer's faith in action is absolutely necessary to connect the authority of Jesus Christ with the power of the Holy Spirit to engage in destroying the works of the devil and to expand the kingdom of God on earth. In order to create God's miracle zone around us, we must mix our faith with the authority of Jesus Christ and the power of the Holy Spirit (Faith + Authority + Power → Miracle). Therefore, the true barometer that needs to be used for anyone who is truly baptized with the Holy Spirit must not solely rest on his ability to speak with new tongues. But he must bear fruit worthy of becoming the witness of Jesus Christ from his own Jerusalem to the ends of the earth, utilizing the authority of Jesus Christ and the power of the Holy Spirit to destroy the works of the devil.

Now we can examine John 16:8-11 more closely:
He will convict the world...

Of Sin: "*...of sin, because they do not believe in Me (Jesus Christ)*" (John 16:9). The primary purpose of the Holy Spirit is to convict the world of its sin, so that the world might be saved through having faith in Jesus Christ. The main issue of all human problems lies in the root of sin. Therefore Isaiah 59:1-2 describes, "*Behold, the Lord's hand is not shortened, that it cannot save; nor His ear heavy, that it cannot hear. But your iniquities have separated you from your God; and your sins have hidden His face from you, so that He will not hear.*" Since the first man, Adam, sinned before God, man tried to hide from the presence of the Lord (Genesis 3:10). However, it was God who first sought after the lost sinner in Genesis 3:9: "*Then the Lord God called to Adam and said to him, 'Where are you?'*" God is still calling sinners to repent of their sins and to come back to Him through the convicting voice of the Holy Spirit.

Of Righteousness: "*...of righteousness, because I go to My Father and you see Me no more*" (John 16:10). The sinners can only be saved through the righteousness of Jesus Christ. We are only able to stand before God if the blood of Jesus Christ has washed our sins away. The Holy Spirit will empower us to minister the righteousness of Jesus Christ to the lost souls in the world. It is not by our own righteousness that we can earn the merits to enter into the kingdom of heaven. By simply accepting the righteous act of God that He accomplished on the cross to take away the sin of the world will open the door for whosoever calls upon the name of the Lord Jesus Christ to be saved.

Of Judgment: "*...of judgment, because the ruler of this world is judged* (John 16:11)." Satan's head was crushed just as God promised in Genesis 3:15 when Jesus Christ rose from the dead as the Lion of Judah. Now all authority in heaven and on earth has been given to Jesus Christ. This means Satan has no authority in heaven and on earth. Therefore, believers in Christ have authority over Satan and the power over darkness through faith in the name of Jesus Christ and by the power of the Holy Spirit. *"Most assuredly, I say to you, he who believes in Me, the works that I do he will do also; and greater works than these he will do, because I go to My Father* (John 14:12).*"*

In order for the children of God to convict the world of sin, righteousness, and judgment, we must read the Bible daily, pray without ceasing, be filled with the Holy Spirit each day, and bring the kingdom of God on the earth by preaching the gospel and declaring the kingdom power according to the commandment in Matthew 10:7-8. You will be known by the fruit that you will bear each day for His glory.

THE MAIN FUNCTION OF
THE HOLY SPIRIT

Jesus Christ describes the most important function of the Holy Spirit when the Spirit came upon the believer in John 16:13-15:

To guide believers into all truth: *"When He, the Spirit of truth, has come, He will* **guide** *you into all truth* (John 16:13).*"* Once the Holy Spirit comes down upon you, He will guide you into all truth so that you will not be misguided by evil and unclean spirits of the devil as well as your own human spirit. In order for the Holy Spirit to guide you well, you need to have a constant two-way communication with Him. The Holy Spirit is the Guide of your life. Therefore, the very success of your mission in life will be absolutely dependent on your reliance on Him to guide your life each step of the way—for small as well as big matters in life. If you rely on the guidance of the Holy Spirit for everything in your life, then whatever you do will always glorify Jesus Christ and fulfill the will of the Father God. Then, you will become a mighty man or woman of God.

To hear from Him: He will speak to you: "*For He will not speak on His own authority, but whatever He hears He will speak (to you)* (John 16: 13b)." Not only the Holy Spirit will guide you with His divine wisdom and power but also He will speak to you whatever He hears from the Father God and Jesus Christ about you.

The Holy Spirit is the direct line to the throne room of God in heaven and only through Him; you will know the perfect will of God for your life. Therefore, if He speaks to you, then you must listen carefully for what He has to say to you. It is better to hear His voice for two minutes than to pray to God for a thousand hours without knowing or hearing the reply from the Lord through the Holy Spirit.

To tell believers things to come: "*He will tell you things to come* (John 16:13b)." In the Old Testament days, God used His prophets to tell His people things to come. Now, in the New Covenant, God, the Holy Spirit, who knows all things of the past, present, and future will directly tell you things to come. You do not need any other mediator between Jesus Christ and you except the Holy Spirit. Through prayers and the daily communion with the Holy Spirit, you will be able to know what is yet to come in your life. When the Spirit of the Living God provides you with His divine insight about the things to come, you can trust Him at His word.

To glorify Jesus Christ: "*He will glorify Me, for He will take of what is Mine and declare it to you* (John 16:14)." According to this verse, whatever you hear from the Holy Spirit will always glorify Jesus Christ because He will take of what is Christ's and declare it to you. Whatever you hear from the Holy Spirit will always be in line with the perfect will of Jesus Christ and the word of God. Therefore, whatever you thought that you heard from the Holy Spirit that does not glorify Jesus Christ, was probably received from your own spirit or from the angel of light—the devil. The Holy Spirit will take that which is exactly of Jesus Christ and declare it to you. We need to develop our listening ears for the still, small voice of the Holy Spirit at all times. Once we know the perfect will of God through the Holy Spirit, then we need to obey and give all the glory to Jesus Christ for any fruit that we may bear.

To testify of Jesus Christ: *"The Spirit of truth who proceeds from the Father, He will testify of Me* (John 15:26)." According to this verse, the Spirit of Truth will proceed from the Father to testify of Jesus Christ. Therefore, we can conclude that Jesus Christ came to this world to glorify and to obey the perfect will of the Father God. The Holy Spirit came to you so that He can testify of Jesus Christ through you. In order for you to testify of Jesus Christ in your life, the Holy Spirit had to come to empower you so that you can be the witness of Him according to Acts 1:8. God, the Holy Spirit, wants you to exercise the authority of Jesus Christ to destroy the works of the devil from your Jerusalem to the ends of the earth.

As you obey and do what Jesus Christ has called and anointed you to do, the signs, wonders, and miracles of the Holy Spirit will follow you to testify of Jesus Christ in your life to the lost souls in the world. The Apostle Paul directs us in 2 Corinthians 13:14 that we ought to have communion (Greek: *Koinonia*) with the Holy Spirit. To have fellowship with the Holy Spirit, we must constantly talk to Him so that we can hear the voice, mind, and will of God through the Holy Spirit. The functions of the Holy Spirit emphasize that

He wants to **guide** us, **speak** to us, **tell** us to **glorify** the Lord, **declare** to us what is of God, and **testify** of Jesus Christ to the world through us. If these are truly His desires for the temples of the Holy Spirit, then we must listen to His still small voice in all things that we do in Christ's name.

Koinonia contains three active meanings: 1) fellowship, 2) participation, and 3) impartation. Firstly, John 16:13-15 describes the importance of the **fellowship** with the Holy Spirit. We need to include the Holy Spirit in every aspect of life as our Divine Helper. If a man is married to a woman, then he needs to include his wife as his helper to have fellowship in the journey of his married life. As a believer honors the Holy Spirit as his Divine Helper in life, he can truly declare that *"With God, all things are possible in my life."* Secondly, Jesus' command in Matthew 10:7-8 depicts the aspect of **participation** in the work of Jesus Christ. If we are led by the Holy Spirit, then we are commanded and empowered to preach the kingdom of heaven wherever we go just like Jesus Christ did.

Not only that we are also commissioned to heal the sick, cleanse the lepers, raise the dead, and cast out demons as the witnesses of Jesus Christ on the earth. God, the Holy Spirit, will assist us to take part in the same ministry of Jesus Christ as His special agents. Thirdly, 2 Timothy 2:2 says, *"And the things that you have heard from me among many witnesses, commit these to faithful men who will be able to teach others also."*

This indicates the **impartation** aspect of *koinonia*. Once we partake in fellowship and participation of the Holy Spirit in our ministry and lives, then we also need to impart what we have gained to other disciples. The Holy Spirit wants to disciple other children of God through you by imparting what you have learned from Him. We are called to make disciples of all the nations. God, the Holy Spirit, really wants to have an intimate *koinonia* with us, so that we will be able to know and understand the perfect will of God to become His mighty witnesses in the world for His glory.

THE TEMPLE OF THE HOLY SPIRIT

In the Old Testament, when Moses finished building the Tabernacle according to the exact measurements in Exodus 40:34-35, he was not able to enter into it because the glory of the Lord filled the Tabernacle. Also, when King Solomon finished the Temple according to the direction that was given to King David, his father, in 1 Kings 8:10-11, the priests could not continue ministering because the glory of the Lord filled the house of the Lord. What separated the Temple of the Lord from any other man-made temples in the world was the glory of God that indwelled in His holy Temple.

Once the Temple was established in the Old Testament days, God commanded the high priest to offer animal sacrifices to atone for the sins of the Israelites in accordance with the laws written in the book of Leviticus. The blood of the lamb was perpetually applied on the altar of the Temple. Now under the New Covenant, the Son of the Living God, Jesus Christ, was sacrificed as the Lamb of God once and forever for the sin of the world. He is the Mediator of the New Covenant, according to Hebrews 9:11-15:

> *But Christ came as High Priest of the good things to come, with the greater and more perfect tabernacle not made with hands, that is, not of this creation. Not with the blood of goats and calves, but with His own blood He entered the Most Holy Place once for all, having obtained eternal redemption. For if the blood*

of bulls and goats and the ashes of a heifer, sprinkling the unclean, sanctifies for the purifying of the flesh, how much more shall the blood of Christ, who through the eternal Spirit offered Himself without spot to God, cleanse your conscience from dead works to serve the living God? And for this reason He is the Mediator of the new covenant, by means of death, for the redemption of the transgressions under the first covenant, that those who are called may receive the promise of the eternal inheritance.

Through the blood of the Lamb of God, we can boldly come to the throne of grace, the very throne of God (the Most Holy Place) in heaven (Hebrews 4:16). Therefore, as we accept Jesus Christ as our Lord and Savior, we are in a way symbolically applying His blood on our heart where Christ indwells for the remission of sin.

As we become a believer and fulfill the requirement of the New Covenant in Christ, then our body becomes the New Temple of the Holy Spirit, according to 1 Corinthians 6:19-20, *"Do you not know that your body is the temple of the Holy Spirit who is in you, whom you have from God, and you are not your own? For you were bought at a price; therefore glorify God in your body and in your spirit, which are God's."*

When the Old Covenant Temple was finished in 1 Kings 8:10,11, God filled the Temple with His glory. Likewise, after the sacrificial death, resurrection, and ascension of Jesus Christ was accomplished, He was glorified and sent the Holy Spirit, the promise of His Father (Luke 24:49), upon every believer. He filled the New Covenant temples (promised children of Abraham, believers in Christ, the Church) with the glory of God (Acts 2). Believers were baptized with the Holy Spirit according to the promise in Matthew 3:11, *"He will baptize you with the Holy Spirit and fire."* This is the direct fulfillment of God's prophecy in Jeremiah 31:31-34, which is also quoted in Hebrews 8:7-13, *"I will put My laws in their mind and write them on their hearts; and I will be their God, and they will be My people* (Hebrews 8:10)."

WHY DO WE NEED TO BE FILLED WITH THE HOLY SPIRIT?

The Temple of God must be filled with the glory of God: Once again, just as the glory of God filled the Old Covenant Temple, the New Covenant temples (Believers in Christ) also need to be filled with His glory (the Holy Spirit). What set the Old Testament Temple apart from other religious temples of the world was that the tangible presence of the glory of God dwelt in it. The Israelites were worshipers not of the man-made idols in the Temple but of the presence of God in His purest form of glory.

Likewise, the new living temples of God must also be filled with the glory of God and the indwelling presence of the Holy Spirit. This was prophesied throughout the Old Testament in Isaiah 44:3, Ezekiel 39:29, and Joel 2:28-32. The glorified Jesus Christ was able to fulfill the Old Testament prophecies (the promise of the Father) as He sent the Holy Spirit upon the believer.

Therefore, the Bible declares in Romans 8:9, *"Now if anyone does not have the Spirit of Christ, he is not His."* The indwelling presence and glory of God through the presence of the Spirit in a believer qualifies him to become a New Covenant temple—a living stone, according to 1 Peter 2:5, *"you also, as living stones, are being built up a spiritual house, a holy priesthood, to offer up spiritual sacrifices acceptable to God through Jesus Christ."*

To be witnesses of Jesus Christ: It is very important to re-address this point. When we become born-again believers in Christ, the Holy Spirit comes in and seals us as the guarantee of our inheritance in the kingdom of heaven (Ephesians 1:13-14). In a way, the initial sealing of the Holy Spirit elevates a believer's position to sit together in the heavenly places in Christ Jesus (Ephesians 2:6). However, when Jesus Christ baptizes us with the Holy Spirit, He brings the kingdom of heaven down to the earth with the power of the Holy Spirit. The Holy Spirit upon a believer will empower him/her to become the witness of Jesus Christ from his/her own Jerusalem to the end of the earth to fulfill Matthew 28:18-20.

Chapter 11

THE KINGDOM OF HEAVEN IS AT HAND

⁓

The first recorded preaching in the New Testament is the voice of John the Baptist in Matthew 3:2, "*Repent, for the kingdom of heaven is at hand!*" The messages of the Old and New Testaments are all about God's kingdom on earth with His chosen people (Israelites—physical descendants of Abraham) in the Old Testament, and the new temples of the Holy Spirit (spiritual children of Abraham) in the New Testament. After Jesus Christ fasted forty days and forty nights and overcame the temptation of the devil, He preached His first message in Matthew 4:17, "*Repent, for the kingdom of heaven is at hand.*" Jesus Christ came to reestablish the invisible reign and rule of the kingdom of heaven on the earth as the King of Kings and the Lord of Lords.

When Adam lost his authority to have dominion over all the earth to the devil, he lost the kingdom of heaven that was extended unto him with its full benefits, anointing, authority and power to rule the earth. As the devil usurped the first Adam's authority to have dominion over the earth, he became the ruler of this world (John 16:11). After the fall of Adam, as mentioned earlier, God's curses were activated upon this earth. God first cursed the serpent (Satan or the devil) in

Genesis 3:14, *"Because you have done this, you are cursed more than all cattle, and more than every beast of the field."* Secondly, God cursed the ground for the sake of Adam and declared, *"In the sweat of your face you shall eat bread till you return to the ground."* Also, God punished Eve, the woman, in Genesis 3:16, *"I will greatly multiply your sorrow and your conception; in pain you shall bring forth children; your desire shall be for your husband, and he shall rule over you."* Thirdly, God cursed Cain who killed his own brother, Abel, in Genesis 4:11-12, *"So now you are cursed from the earth, which has opened its mouth to receive your brother's blood cries out to Me from the ground. When you till the ground, it shall no longer yield its strength to you. A fugitive and a vagabond you shall be on the earth."*

Therefore, sin brought God's curses upon the earth and Satan became the ruler of this cursed world. Sin opened the door to invite diseases, curses, death, and Satan's wicked and evil temptations upon the whole humanity. The whole world became corrupted with sin which caused God to destroy man from the face of the earth in Noah's days in Genesis 6:5-7, *"Then the Lord saw that the wickedness of man was great in the earth, and that every intent of the thoughts of his heart was only evil continually. And the Lord was sorry that He had made man on the earth, and He was grieved in His heart. So the Lord said, 'I will destroy man whom I have created from the face of the earth, both man and beast, creeping thing and birds of the air, for I am sorry that I have made them."* Only Noah and his family of eight and selected clean and unclean male and female animals found the grace and mercy of God to be spared from His divine judgment by the Flood.

The primary work of the devil in this world is to instill his wicked schemes of manipulation, lies, and deception into the heart of fallen mankind so that whosoever falls into his trap will invoke God's curses upon himself. John 8:44b describes

Satan's immoral character: *"He was a murderer from the beginning, and does not stand in the truth, because there is no truth in him. When he speaks a lie, he speaks from his own resources, for he is a liar and the father of it."* **The devil will entice anyone not to forgive the sins of others** by manipulating the person to believe that he has every right to judge, condemn, or criticize the offender. Once anyone falls into committing unforgiveness and bitterness, then God's judgment of Matthew 6:14-15 will come upon him: *"For if you forgive men their trespasses, your heavenly Father will also forgive you. But if you do not forgive men their trespasses, neither will your Father forgive your trespasses."*

Furthermore, a person will be delivered unto torturers, according to Jesus' illustration about "an unforgiving servant" in Matthew 18:23-35, *"Then his master, after he had called him, said to him, 'You wicked servant! I forgave you all that debt because you begged me. Should you not also have had compassion on your fellow servant, just as I had a pity on you?' And his master was angry, and delivered him to the torturers (the devil and his demons) until he should pay all that was due to him. So **My heavenly Father also will do to you if each of you, from his heart, does not forgive his brother his trespasses**."* Sin will give the devil legal rights to torture victims backed by the word of God.

Just like the law of gravity, a spiritual gravity law also exists. Jesus Christ warns believers not to judge others as Matthew 7:1-2 states: *"**Judge not, that you be not judged. For with what judgment you judge, you will be judged; and with the measure you use, it will be measured back to you.**"* Whatever you judge and condemn others about will eventually roll right back on you with vengeance. I have witnessed a son who used to severely judge his father's alcoholism, later in life, become two times worse of an alcoholic than his father. Why? The son's judgment of his father's problem without mercy allowed the devil to have a legal right to attack him with the double portion of judgment and curse. We must not judge others based on our own understanding of their situation but allow God to be the Judge of their lives according to His righteousness judgment. We need to pray for them so that God's mercy can flow upon them.

One of God's Ten Commandments in Exodus 20:12 says, *"**Honor your father and your mother**, that your days may be long upon the land which the Lord your God is giving you."* The same Commandment was repeated in Ephesians 6:2-3. The consequence of breaking this law may cause a person's life to be potentially shortened on the earth. Dishonoring your parents normally involves harboring unforgiveness and a judgmental spirit against them. As you dishonor, you will reap triple jeopardy consequences: 1) God will not forgive your sins as you are not forgiving your parents' sins. 2) God will judge you with the same measure that you use against your parents. 3) Your sins of unforgiveness, judgmental spirit and dishonoring your parents can prevent blessings and a long life for you on the earth.

All three consequences of sins can fall on their lives until they truly repent. Honoring one's parents (including father and mother-in-laws) does not mean that you condone the wrong they have done to you. However how horrible your parents might have been to you when you were growing up, you, as a born-again Christian, must pray for them, respect them with the love of God, and allow the Lord to be the Judge over their lives. After all, were it not for them, you would not exist on this earth.

To honor your parents means *"regard parents with great respect."* The word "honor" in Exodus 20:12 implies acknowledgment of a person's right to such respect. Over the past 32 years of full-time mission work in the world, I have counseled children who have dishonored their parents. These same children had also experienced minor to severe attacks in their health, relationships, finances and emotional areas by the power of darkness. Therefore, in order for anyone to receive the kingdom of heaven and all of its blessings and benefits on earth, he must repent of sins and turn away from wicked ways. Repentance, humility, and obedience to the word of God will always unlock God's divine blessings in life. So, we must not break God's spiritual gravity laws.

JESUS CAME TO RE-ESTABLISH THE KINGDOM OF GOD ON EARTH

The last Adam came to the world as the Son of Man to destroy the works of the devil (1 John 3:8) and to take away his authority as the ruler of this world (Matthew 28:18). The first Adam's sin brought death to all men but the last Adam's obedience and sacrificial death on the cross opened the door for all men to receive the free gift of God—the abundant life on the earth and eternal life in the kingdom of God forever. Thus, Romans 5:8-19 describes this principle very clearly:

But God demonstrates His own love toward us, in that while we were still sinners, Christ died for us. Much more then, having now been justified by His blood, we shall be saved from wrath through Him. For if when we were enemies we were reconciled to God through the death of His Son, much more, having been reconciled, we shall be saved by His life. And not only that, but we also rejoice in God through our Lord Jesus Christ, through whom we have now received the reconciliation. Therefore, just as through one man sin entered the world, and death through sin, and thus death spread to all men, because all sinned—(For until the law sin was in the world, but sin is not imputed when there is no law. Nevertheless death reigned from Adam to Moses, even over those who had not sinned according to the likeness of the transgression of Adam, who is a type of Him who was to come. But the free gift is not like the offense. ***For if by the one man's offense many died, much more the grace of God and the gift by the grace of the one Man, Jesus Christ, abounded to many.*** *And the gift is not like that which came through the one who sinned. For the judgment which came from one offense resulted in condemnation, but the free gift which came from many offenses resulted in justification.* ***For if by the one man's offense death reigned through the one, much more those who receive abundance of grace and of the gift of righteousness will reign in life through the One, Jesus Christ.****) Therefore, as through one man's offense judgment came to all men, resulting in condemnation, even so through one Man's righteous act the free gift came to all men, resulting in justification of life. For as by one man's disobedience many were made sinners, so also by one Man's obedience many will be made righteous.*

Therefore, Jesus Christ not only came to provide His divine salvation to fallen mankind but also to establish the kingdom of heaven on earth through His chosen people of God. There are more than two hundred political nations in the world. Each of these nations has its own constitution, common language, customs, and culture that govern the welfare of its people and provide special benefits to its citizens. Since the day of Pentecost, the kingdom of heaven has been invading all different peoples, tongues, tribes and nations in the world. The kingdom of heaven on earth has Jesus Christ as the King of Kings and the Lord of Lords; it has the Bible as its constitution and the Holy Spirit as its Governor. The kingdom of heaven has its own benefits for its citizens, according to Psalm 68:19, "*Blessed be the Lord, who daily loads us with benefits, the God of our salvation!*" The Holy Spirit loads us with His daily benefits (Psalm 103:1-5) so that we can be the witness of Jesus Christ to share His divine salvation plan with fallen humanity and demonstrate His kingdom plan to set the lost, dying, and hurting souls free in the world from the power and works of the devil.

In the kingdom of God, King Jesus has His divine authority over every matter on earth and the Holy Spirit can release kingdom power to demolish the stronghold of the devil in any nation, people, tongue and tribe. God will work with His chosen children (Christians) to destroy the works of the devil on earth. The law of the Bible overrides the law of any nation, people, tongue and tribe. The Bible culture is the supra-culture that can also rescind any unholy culture of the world. Therefore, Jesus Christ came not only to provide salvation to lost sinners, but also to transform the evil culture of fallen mankind by establishing the kingdom of heaven on earth.

The citizens of the kingdom of heaven have to abide by God's statutes, laws, regulations, culture, customs and commandment of the constitution of the kingdom in order to enjoy His blessings. Therefore, Jesus Christ not only preached the message of the kingdom of heaven but also demonstrated the kingdom power to heal the sick, cleanse the lepers, raise the dead, and cast out demons wherever He went. Now, Jesus Christ is continuously present through the Holy Spirit who indwells in His disciples to do the same works that Jesus did and even greater works than what He had done. Jesus Christ can only empower His disciples to transform the lost souls who are residing in this cursed world to receive His divine kingdom benefits of abundant life on earth and eternal life in heaven.

Chapter 12

TO THE END OF THE EARTH

⤜✦⤏

The Bible is the story of God's mission work through His chosen people from Genesis to Revelation. In Genesis 12:3, God said to Abram, "*In you all the families of the earth shall be blessed.*" Before God ever created His own special people group, the Israelites, He made His mission very clear to Abraham, the Father of the Jews. The very reason that God called Abraham was to use him and his family to bless all the families of the earth. Throughout the Old Testament, God reiterates His divine purpose of creating the Israelites to shine His light to the Gentiles in the world:

> *I, the LORD, have called You in righteousness, And will hold Your hand;* **I will keep You and give You as a covenant to the people, as a light to the Gentiles,** *to open blind eyes, to bring out prisoners from the prison, those who sit in darkness from the prison house. I am the LORD, that is My name; and My glory I will not give to another, nor My praise to carved image.* (Isaiah 42:6-8)
>
> *I will also* **give You as a light to the Gentiles,** *that You should be My salvation to the ends of the earth.* (Isaiah 49:6b)

*For from the rising of the sun, even to its going down, My name shall be great among the Gentiles; in every place incense shall be offered to My name, and a pure offering; "**For My name shall be great among the nations**," Says the* LORD *of hosts.*   (Malachi 1:11)

God's divine purpose of creating the Israelites was to utilize them as the light to the Gentiles. So, then, who are the children of Abraham? In Galatians 3:7-8, we read, "*Therefore know that only those who are of faith are sons of Abraham. And the Scripture, foreseeing that God would justify the nations by faith, preached the gospel to Abraham beforehand, saying, 'In you all the nations shall be blessed.'*"

According to these Scriptures, those who are of faith are sons of Abraham. We, the Church, the Body of Christ, are adopted spiritual sons of Abraham. The call of Abraham in Genesis 12:3 directs every believer in Christ to be a blessing to all the families of the earth. The Church is not the physical building where believers gather on Sundays, but it consists of believing saints—the temples of the Holy Spirit—that are called out of darkness into His marvelous light. They are the living temples of the Lord on this earth where the Holy Spirit dwells.

WHO HAS THE KEYS OF THE KINGDOM OF HEAVEN?

Jesus Christ declared to Peter after he made the true confession of who Jesus was in Matthew 16:18-19, "*Now I say to you that you are Peter (which means 'rock'), and upon this rock I will build my church, and all the powers of hell will not conquer it. And I will give you **the keys of the Kingdom*** *of Heaven. Whatever you forbid on earth will be forbidden in heaven, and whatever you permit on earth will be permitted in heaven.* (NLT)" Jesus Christ is the Master Key of the kingdom of heaven, and He gave the duplicate keys of the kingdom of heaven to His Church. Each and every born-again believer of Jesus Christ in the Church is a key of the kingdom of heaven. Believers are the only ones who know the gospel of Jesus Christ and the way to the kingdom of heaven. Therefore, if a Christian is a key to the kingdom of heaven, he must do everything possible in his power to unlock the devil's chains upon the people of this world through preaching the salvation plan of God and demonstrating the kingdom plan wherever he goes.

Jesus Christ has become the Judge of the living and the dead, and He holds the keys of Hades and of Death, according to Revelation 1:18, *"I am He who lives, and was dead, and behold, I am alive forevermore, Amen. And I have the keys of Hades and Death."* Therefore, Satan has neither authority on earth nor the keys of Hades and death. Christ has the power to cast the devil, the beast, the false prophet and anyone not found written in the Book of Life into the lake of fire according to Revelation 20:10-15.

The Bible declares in Hebrews 9:27, *"And as it is appointed for men to die once, but after this the judgment."* Once we die, Jesus Christ, the Great Judge, will judge every soul according to his own works. Therefore, Jesus Christ can declare in John 14:6, *"I am the way, the truth, and the life. No one comes to the Father except through Me."* If a person's sins have not been washed by the blood of the Lamb, he or she has to pay the penalty of his or her sins forever in the lake of fire according to Revelation 20:15. Therefore, we must do everything that we can to preach the gospel to save the lost souls in the world. Fulfilling the Great Commission has to be our first love for Jesus Christ.

MAKE DISCIPLES OF ALL THE NATIONS

The main call of the Great Commission is to make disciples of Jesus Christ from the nations of the world:

> *All authority has been given to Me in heaven and on earth. "Go therefore and **make disciples of all the nations**, baptizing them in the name of the Father and of the Son and of the Holy Spirit, teaching them to observe all things that I have commanded you; and lo, I am with you always, even to the end of the age."*
>
> (Matthew 28:18-20)

In the original Greek text, the commands of going, baptizing, and teaching in Matthew 28:19-20 are all participles which support the main verb "making" disciples. Thus, the most important aspect of any ministry and mission is to make disciples of Jesus Christ in order to evangelize the world for His glory. According to Merriam-Webster's Online Dictionary, the term "disciple" means: *"one who accepts and assists in spreading the doctrines of another as one of the twelve in the inner circle of Christ's followers according to the Gospel accounts."* A born-again believer will normally accept the teaching and doctrine of the gospel. However, only true disciples of Jesus Christ will not only accept the doctrine but also assist in spreading the gospel in order to make more disciples by obeying the Great Commission in Matthew 28:18-20 and Acts 1:8. Let's look at two important principles of making disciples in the world:

Indigenous Training Principle: Missions mobilizers from evangelized countries must equip national or indigenous leaders in their own mission fields to create true disciples of Jesus Christ who will, in turn, train others to assist in

216

spreading the kingdom of God among their own unreached people groups. Melvin Hodges who wrote *"Why Indigenous Church Principles?"* states, *"The word indigenous means that, as a result of missionary effort, a national ministry has been produced which shares the life of the country in which it's planted and finds within itself the ability to govern itself, support itself, and reproduce itself."* Therefore, any foreign missionaries must create "Indigenous Missions Movement" to spread the kingdom of God in their mission fields by equipping national leaders to create self-governing, self-supporting, and self-propagating national missions and churches.

Contextualization Principle: The equipped indigenous leaders train lay leaders to plant contextualized churches. Steven Hawthorne who is one of the renowned teachers of missiology best describes contextualized church planting: *"A contextualized church is both Biblical and culturally authentic. It is viable insofar as it displays Biblical vitality. It is indigenous insofar as the cultural and social patterns it espouses, arise from and speak to its own culture. Because of this spiritual and cultural authenticity, a contextualized church is most often found to be an evangelizing church which could accurately be described as a Christian Movement."*

Therefore, any foreign missionaries must not create any mission churches to follow the pattern, culture, custom, and style of their own home churches. But they must plant culturally authentic and indigenous mission churches which represent the pattern, culture, custom, and style of mission fields as long as they display Biblical vitality.

It is very important that Western mission forces do not create a "franchise" style of denominational churches that impart colonial style domination, control, and flavor. Mission churches must be planted by the trained national leaders and not implanted by foreign missionaries. The trained indigenous leaders must implement the indigenous discipleship training method as well as contextualization principles to usher in the Holy Spirit movement among their own unreached people groups.

WHEN WILL THE END COME?

Jesus Christ declares in Matthew 24:14, *"And this gospel of the kingdom will be preached in all the world as a witness to all the **nations**, and then the end will come."* When 4,588 unreached people groups (the most current report by Joshua Project: July 2020) in the world have a chance to hear the Gospel of Jesus Christ, then the end will come and Jesus Christ will come back to establish His eternal kingdom on earth. The prophecy of Revelation 11:15b will be fulfilled: *"The kingdoms of this world have become the kingdoms of our Lord and of His Christ, and He shall reign forever and ever!"* The prophecy of Daniel 2:44 will also come to pass: *"And in the days of these kings the God of heaven will set up a kingdom which shall never be destroyed; and the kingdom shall not be left to other people; it shall break in pieces and consume all these kingdoms, and it shall stand forever."*

Therefore, the end will come when the Church of the Living God in the Western world, as well as the rest of the world, will take the Great Commission in Matthew 28:18-20 and Acts 1:8 seriously and spread the gospel to every unengaged and unreached people group in the world. The world mission's strategy of Western churches must be dramatically changed in order to expedite the process of bringing the closure to the Great Commission in Matthew 24:14.

A typical Western mission's strategy is to physically mobilize Western long-term missionaries by assigning them to unreached people groups in the world. The next step is that they must learn indigenous languages, cultures, customs and value systems that can easily take three-to-five years for a missionary. Only after mastering the enculturation of an indigenous people group, a missionary can effectively begin to evangelize an unreached people group. With the typical missions' approach, it normally takes a long time for a Western missionary to penetrate into an unreached people group with the gospel of Jesus Christ. Instead of following the above traditional approach, the Western missionaries must become missions' mobilizers to locate and identify viable indigenous Christians and local churches that have been planted in close proximity to the unreached people groups.

Once Western missionaries identify them, then they need to train and equip native leaders of the evangelized people groups to become indigenous mission forces. These indigenous missionaries are much more familiar with the culture, customs, languages and value system of the adjacent unreached people groups. Western mission's mobilizers need to equip indigenous leaders to raise their own mission forces that will spread the message of the kingdom of God among the identified unreached people groups by implementing an indigenous church planting movement.

When a viable indigenous church (that is self-governing, self-supporting and self-propagating within its own cultural group) has been planted in an unreached people group by trained indigenous missionaries, then the Western mission's mobilizers must turn the ministry over to the indigenous church leaders. However, Western mission's mobilizers can provide the necessary advice, further trainings and assistance to native leaders as a partnering ministry. Once the transfer of the ministry to indigenous leaders has accomplished, Western missionaries need to move their missions into other evangelized indigenous regions to equip the native disciples to target other unreached people groups. The Western mission's mobilizers may not need to stay in the evangelized region for a long period of time. They could travel to the region with a short-term trained mission team to establish an indigenous Missions Training Center—an intensive discipleship training program that must be operated and managed by indigenous teachers and leaders. Once native Christian missionaries have been raised, they in turn need to launch an indigenous mission's movement to evangelize their own unengaged and unreached people groups.

The Western missions must concentrate on mobilizing indigenous mission forces among evangelized people groups that are inhabited within the close proximity to unreached people groups in the world. In turn, trained indigenous missions forces need to bring the kingdom messages into the unreached people groups. Through launching the indigenous mission movements, we may truly witness the whole 4,392 unreached people groups will hear the gospel of the kingdom of God within the next twenty years. If that happens, the end will come soon and we can say, "Maranatha! Come Lord Jesus Christ!"

GOD'S ORDER OF BUSINESS

When God gave the Great Commission in Acts 1:8 and Matthew 28:18-20 to His disciples, the Holy Spirit had not yet come down upon the believers, and the first Jerusalem church was not even in their minds. However, they clearly understood that the foremost call upon their lives was to fulfill the Great Commission. Therefore, Jesus Christ baptized the first one hundred and twenty disciples with the power of the Holy Spirit in Acts 2 so that He could empower them to fulfill the Great Commission and Matthew 24:14.

At the same time, the Holy Spirit helped the believers to form the Church as the means to fulfill the end—global evangelization. Therefore, the two most important aspects of the ministries of the Church are the evangelization of the lost souls within its own Jerusalem, Judea, and Samaria and the world missions to the ends of the earth. All other departments such as finance, personnel, worship, children, youth, Sunday schools, home groups, and others in a church should be the supporting parts to fulfill God's Great Commission (the call of God for His Church). A church must constantly evangelize the local area as well as send world mission's team to equip native leaders to plant indigenous churches among unreached people groups in the world. The following diagram illustrates God's plan for the world:

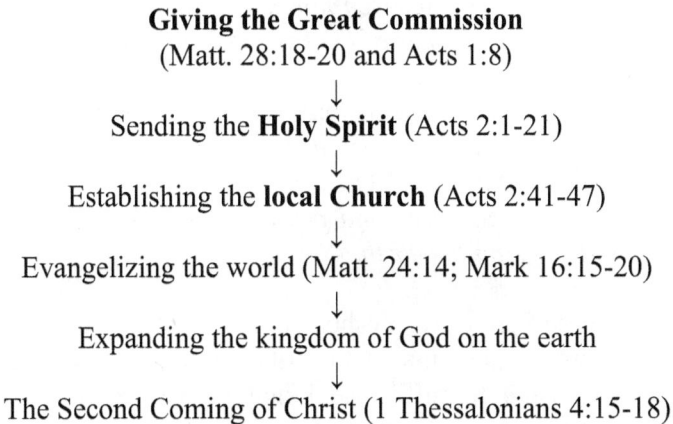

Giving the Great Commission
(Matt. 28:18-20 and Acts 1:8)
↓
Sending the **Holy Spirit** (Acts 2:1-21)
↓
Establishing the **local Church** (Acts 2:41-47)
↓
Evangelizing the world (Matt. 24:14; Mark 16:15-20)
↓
Expanding the kingdom of God on the earth
↓
The Second Coming of Christ (1 Thessalonians 4:15-18)

TO EVERY TRIBE AND TONGUE AND PEOPLE AND NATION

From the call of Abraham in Genesis 12:1-3, God Almighty had His divine plan to utilize His chosen people as the blessing to all the families of the earth so that every tribe and tongue and people and nation will hear the gospel of Jesus Christ. The ultimate will of God for all the families of the earth is clearly described in Revelation 5:5-6; 9-10:

> *But one of the elders said to me, 'Do not weep. Behold, **the Lion of the tribe of Judah**, the Root of David, has prevailed to open the scroll and to loose its seven seals.' And I looked, and behold, in the midst of the throne and of the four living creatures, and in the midst of the elders, stood a **Lamb** as though it had been slain, having seven horns and seven eyes, which are the seven Spirits of God sent out into all the earth. And they sang a new song, saying: 'You are worthy to take the scroll, and to open its seals; for You were slain, and have redeemed us to God by Your blood out of **every tribe and tongue and people and nation**, and have made us kings and priests to our God; and we shall reign on the earth.*

In these Scriptures, Yeshua Ha-Mashiach (Jesus Christ) is recognized as the Lion of the tribe of Judah as well as the Lamb of God, to fulfill the kingdom plan as well as the salvation plan of God through His disciples on the earth. He is the Son of David (Lion of Judah) as well as the Son of Abraham (Lamb of God), the fulfillment of the Old Testament and the Initiator of the New Covenant, according to Matthew 1:1.

However, the most important part of God's prophetic word in the Scriptures can be summed up in His purpose and plan for every tribe and tongue and people and nation. It is not His desire that any should perish but that all should come to repentance (2 Peter 3:9). Once again, we can be assured that God's desire is to save those who will hear the gospel of Jesus Christ from all nations, tribes, peoples, and tongues in accordance with Revelation 7:9, *"After these things I looked, and behold, a great multitude which no one could number, of all nations, tribes, peoples, and tongues, standing before the throne and before the Lamb, clothed with white robes, with palm branches in their hands, and crying out with a loud voice, saying, 'Salvation belongs to our God who sits on the throne, and to the Lamb!' "*

Praise the Lord forevermore! One day, when the saints enter into the kingdom of heaven, they will find out that the children of God from every nation, tribe, people, and tongue are represented before the throne and the Lamb of God. Therefore, God has established the Church so that the sons of Abraham will go to every tribe and tongue and people and nation in the name of Jesus Christ to share the Gospel of the kingdom. Then, who will direct this mission? On behalf of Jesus Christ, the Holy Spirit is the Director of His worldwide mission. Who must go for the Lord? You! The Church! The believers! Yes, Christians! Who will support the Great Commission to be fulfilled in our lifetime? Every born-again believer in Christ, who is the temple of the Holy Spirit and who constitutes the local church, must be the means to fulfill the end—the Great Commission. Every church must be involved in supporting the world missions with financial means as well as to dispatch missions' mobilizers into the nations to expand the kingdom of God into the unreached people groups in the world. If you are not called to go, then you must support someone else to go. Together, we can bring the closure to the Great Commission within the next twenty years if we obey His calls in Matthew 28:19-20.

JESUS WILL COME AGAIN

Jesus Christ comforted His disciples as He announced His soon departure in John 14:1-3, *"Let not your heart be troubled; you believe in God, believe also in Me. In My Father's house are many mansions; if it were not so, I would have told you. I go to prepare a place for you. And if I go and prepare a place for you, I will come again and receive you to Myself; that where I am, there you may be also."*

Also, Jesus Christ's Second Coming was reassured in Acts 1:11, *"As Jesus Christ was ascending to heaven, the disciples looked steadfastly toward heaven. Then two angels said to them, 'Men of Galilee, why do you stand gazing up into heaven? This same Jesus, who was taken up from you into heaven, will so come in like manner as you saw Him go into heaven.'"*

Once we, the believers of Jesus Christ (New Testament Church), do our part in preaching the gospel to every ethnic people group (Matthew 24:14) in the world, Jesus Christ will come back as He promised. Jesus Christ will set up His eternal kingdom on earth as the King of Kings and the Lord of Lords. Eventually, this cursed world will become a new earth where there will be no more curses as declared in Revelation 22:3a, *"And there shall be no more curse, but the throne of God and of the Lamb shall be in it, and His servants shall serve Him."*

THE DEAD IN CHRIST WILL BE RAISED FIRST

The Apostle Paul writes in 1 Corinthians 15:51-54 that the dead in Christ will be raised incorruptible: *"Behold, I tell you a mystery: We shall not all sleep, but we shall all be changed—in a moment, in the twinkling of an eye, at the last trumpet. For the trumpet will sound, and the dead will be raised incorruptible, and this mortal must put on immortality. Then death is swallowed up in victory."*

When Adam and Eve sinned before God, the wages of sin brought death upon every human being who would ever live on the earth. Therefore, the last Adam, Jesus Christ, gave His life for the sins of the world so that those who believe in Him will have eternal life. The last enemy that will be destroyed is death (1 Corinthians 15:26). The last Adam became a life-giving Spirit (1 Corinthians 15:45). Through the power of the resurrection of Jesus Christ, those who died in Christ will be raised incorruptible to destroy the sting of death, and those who are alive will never taste death on the day of the second coming of the Lord as described in 1 Corinthians 15:51-54 says.

The same assurance is reinforced in 1 Thessalonians 4:16-17, *"For the Lord Himself will descend from heaven with a shout, with the voice of an archangel, and with the trumpet of God. And the dead in Christ will rise first. Then we who are alive and remain shall be caught up together with them in the clouds to meet the Lord in the air. And thus we shall always be with the Lord"* Our victory in Christ has been sealed with the Holy Spirit when we first believed in Him. The children of God can boldly declare, *"O Death, where is your sting? O Hades, where is your victory? The sting of death is sin, and the strength of sin is the law. But thanks be to God, who gives*

225

us the victory through our Lord Jesus Christ" (1 Corinthians 15:55-57). However, when the disciples asked Jesus Christ, *"Lord, will You at this time restore the kingdom to Israel?"* in Acts 1:6, before His ascension to heaven, He responded in Acts 1:7, *"It is not for you to know times or seasons which the Father has put in His own authority."* Also, the Apostle Paul writes in 1 Thessalonians 5:1-10:

> *But concerning the times and the seasons, brethren, you have no need that I should write to you. For you yourselves know perfectly that the day of the Lord so comes as a thief in the night. For when they say, "Peace and safety!" then sudden destruction comes upon them, as labor pains upon a pregnant woman. And they shall not escape. **But you, brethren, are not in darkness, so that this Day should overtake you as a thief. You are all sons of light and sons of the day.** We are not of the night nor of darkness. Therefore let us not sleep, as others do, but let us watch and be sober. For those who sleep, sleep at night, and those who get drunk are drunk at night. But let us who are of the day be sober, putting on the breastplate of faith and love, and as a helmet the hope of salvation. For God did not appoint us to wrath, but to obtain salvation through our Lord Jesus Christ, who died for us, that whether we wake or sleep, we should live together with Him.*

We must be ready in-season and out-of-season to preach the gospel in our own Jerusalem, Judea, and Samaria as well as to the ends of the earth to share the good news with totally unreached tribes, tongues, peoples, and nations as quickly as we can for His glory. Jesus Christ will come like a thief in the night. Therefore, we, the Church, must not only talk and rejoice about the Second Coming of Christ in the near future but also fulfill the Great Commission as best as we can within our ability and power to change the world. We must not be satisfied with being the Church as usual. We must allow the full power of the Holy Spirit to bring the revival fire back into our church to empower us to bring the gospel of love, hope, future, resurrection, and life to the lost souls with signs, wonders and miracles following.

THE LAKE OF FIRE

At the end of the age, God will cast the devil, the beast, and the false prophet into the lake of fire forever and ever in Revelation 20:10, *"And the devil, who deceived them, was cast into the lake of fire and brimstone where the beast and the false prophet are. And they will be tormented day and night forever and ever."*

The final judgment of God for those whose lives are not in Christ Jesus will be carried out in accordance with the words in Revelation 20:11-15:

> *Then I saw a great white throne and Him who sat on it, from whose face the earth and the heaven fled away. And there was found no place for them. And I saw the dead, small and great, standing before God, and books were opened. And another book was opened, which is the Book of Life. And the dead were judged according to their works, by the things which were written in the books. The sea gave up the dead who were in it, and Death and Hades delivered up the dead who were in them. And they were judged, each one according to his works. Then Death and Hades*

*were cast into the lake of fire. This is the second death. **And anyone not found written in the Book of Life was cast into the lake of fire.***

If you were to die tonight and you were not absolutely sure that you would awaken in the kingdom of heaven, then you need to make sure of your salvation in Christ so that you would miss the lake of fire. The wages of sin will eventually bring physical death in this world and eternal damnation in the lake of fire. If you die with your sins, you will have to pay for your sins eternally in the lake of fire. But if you repent of your sins by believing that Jesus Christ paid your death penalty on the Cross and surrender your life to Him unconditionally, you will be pardoned from paying for your own sins forever in hell; you will be accepted into the kingdom of heaven after your death on this earth.

THE NEW HEAVEN AND EARTH

From the beginning of Creation, it was God's perfect will for His chosen creation, Adam and Eve's descendants, to live in the Garden of Eden (Paradise on the earth). However, sin brought curses of death, sickness, war, famine, poverty, and destruction into this world. But the ultimate plan of God is to bring His chosen people back to the Paradise through the sacrificial death, burial, and resurrection of Jesus Christ. At the end of the ages, God will put His chosen people into the New Heaven and Earth permanently (Rev. 21:1, 3-4):

Now I saw a new heaven and a new earth, for the first heaven and the first earth had passed away. Also there was no more sea. Behold, the tabernacle of God is with men, and He will dwell with them, and they shall be His people, and God Himself will be with them and be their God. And God will wipe away every tear from their eyes; there shall be no more death, nor sorrow, nor crying; and there shall be no more pain, for the former things have passed away.

Once we enter into the New Earth, there shall be no more death, nor sorrow, nor crying and there shall be no more pain, sickness, war, famine, poverty, and destruction. We will enjoy God's presence, love, and fellowship for eternity in His new Paradise.

I AM COMING QUICKLY!

Jesus is coming back soon as the King of Kings and the Lord of Lords according to Revelation 22:12-15, *"And behold, I am coming quickly, and My reward is with Me, to give to everyone according to his work. I am the Alpha and the Omega, the Beginning and the End, the First and the Last. Blessed are those who do His commandments, that they may have the right to the tree of life, and may enter through the gates into the city. But outside are dogs and sorcerers and sexually immoral and murderers and idolaters, and whoever loves and practices a lie."*

As we take part in the Lord's Supper, we are symbolically eating the fruit of the tree of life—Jesus Christ who provides the eternal life back to His chosen saints to rule and reign in the earth with Him. Jesus Christ will take away the curse forever from the New Earth and release a pure river of water of life proceeding from the throne of God and of the Lamb in Revelation 22:1-5, *"And he showed me a pure river of water of life, clear as crystal, proceeding from the throne of God and of the Lamb. In the middle of its street, and on either side of the river, was the tree of life, which bore twelve fruits, each tree yielding its fruit every month. The leaves of the tree were for the healing of the nations. And there shall be no more curse, but the throne of God and of the Lamb shall be in it, and His servants shall serve Him. They shall see His face, and His name shall be on their foreheads. There shall be no night there: they need no lamp nor light of the sun, for the Lord God gives them light. And they shall reign forever and ever."*

Since the resurrection of Jesus Christ, the river of life has been flowing throughout the world. The prophecy of Ezekiel 47:9 has been fulfilled: *"And it shall be that every living thing that moves, wherever the rivers go, will live."* As you come to God's river, your sins will be forgiven, and you shall receive new life with His love, joy, and peace flowing limitlessly.

COME! COME! COME!

Jesus Christ is calling whoever desires to have the water of life in Revelation 22:17, *"And the Spirit and the bride say, 'Come!' And let him who hears say, 'Come!' And let him who thirsts come. And whoever desires, let him take the water of life freely."* God is calling every people and tribe and tongue and nation to come to Him and to receive the tree of life freely. **Receive Yeshua Ha-Mashiach or Jesus Christ as your Lord and Savior and live!** The choice is in your hand as in Deuteronomy 30:19, *"I call heaven and earth as witnesses today against you, that I have set before you life and death, blessing and cursing; therefore choose life, that both you and your descendants may live."* If you choose Jesus Christ as your Lord and Savior right now, the blood of the

Lamb will wash your sins, and He will fill you with the Holy Spirit so that you can be His shining light to bring His salvation, healing, deliverance, and the message of reconciliation to this suffering and dying world. Some day soon, you will inherit the new earth as your eternal Paradise. Come! Come! Come! While there is time, you need to come to Jesus Christ—the Lamb and the Lion of God, the Messiah of the Gentiles of the world and the Israelites. Come! Let us go to the cross of Jesus Christ and repent of our sins. Once we crucify our sins and old man on the cross with Jesus Christ, then we can boldly go through the cross into the kingdom of God as His chosen saints and disciples. With the authority of Jesus Christ and the power of the Holy Spirit residing within us, we can transform the world for His glory during our time on this earth.

AUTHOR'S PRAYER

Oh Lord! I pray that You would bless all peoples, tongues, tribes, and nations who read this book and empower them to find new life in Jesus Christ. May You guide them to the cross of Jesus Christ so that their spiritual eyes will be opened to the true message of the gospel of the kingdom of God. When they repent of their sins, Oh Lord, please forgive their sins and give them abundant life on this earth and eternal life in heaven. May You fill them with the power and anointing of the Holy Spirit and guide them to be Your shining light in this dark world! May you grant them divine life, health and provision so that they can be Your living witnesses in their Jerusalem to the ends of the earth for Your glory! May You protect them and keep them in your hand and bless all they do for You from this time forward and forever more! Amen!

ABOUT THE AUTHOR AND HIS MINISTRY

Dr. James Lee is the Founder and President of River of Life Ministries, whose mission is to equip national Christian leaders through River Mission Training Centers (RMTCs) and Global Harvest Network (GHN) Seminars to plant indigenous churches among unreached people groups in the world. He is also the Founder and President of Door of Hope Foundation, which carries out God's divine mission to bring the hope of Jesus Christ to facilitate charitable works that will enhance the welfare of the neediest and most vulnerable children in the world.

In 1985, James received the call to become a full-time minister while stationed in the Flying Squadron 2 of NATO AWACS base in Germany as a senior Captain in the U.S. Air Force. Since he resigned his commission in the Air Force in 1987, he received his Master of Arts in World Missions and a Doctor of Ministry degree in Global Evangelization from Regent University in Virginia Beach. Since 1988, James has traveled to more than 100 countries spreading the Gospel of Jesus Christ to multitudes of unreached people groups. He has equipped indigenous disciples through establishing the RMTCs and conducting GHN Seminars, and his disciples planted over 800 indigenous churches worldwide. James is an apostle to the nations, anointed evangelist, equipper of disciples, and a gifted preacher with signs, wonders and miracles following in his ministry.

OTHER BOOKS BY DR. JAMES LEE

When God Walks with an Ordinary Man—A book which will inspire all believers in Christ to trust Him with all their heart by allowing Him to walk with them to achieve His plan and purpose in their lives for His glory. God can empower His ordinary sons and daughters with His divine authority and power to accomplish His extraordinary tasks on earth as His special agents.

It is Written—This book will guide sons and daughters of God to do spiritual warfare totally focusing on God and His mighty power instead of concentrating on Satan and His power of darkness. In this book, we will examine the Scriptures to see how the heroes of the faith conducted spiritual warfare so we can learn from their examples on how to apply biblical principles to our own spiritual battles in life.

CONTACT INFORMATION

If God has made this book a blessing to you and you wish to share a testimony, or if you wish to be on the River of Life Ministries' mailing list to become a partner and receive our monthly newsletter, write to:

River of Life Ministries
P. O. Box 6128
Virginia Beach, VA 23456-0128
e-mail: riveroflife@rlmva.org
Web: www.rlmva.org
Tel: 757-554-0053

If you wish to support orphans and needy children in the world, then write to:

Door of Hope Foundation
P. O. Box 6261
Virginia Beach, VA 23456-0261
e-mail: dhf@doorofhopefoundation.com
web: www.doorofhopefoundation.com
Tel: 757-271-6755

www.ingramcontent.com/pod-product-compliance
Lightning Source LLC
Chambersburg PA
CBHW051820090426
42736CB00011B/1578